FERRY
1606
Eight Branches

2
964
33
AND
ONLY
Bunker
1989

INSUR
DAWN
TASCONES
COFFEE SHOP
PECK-JUDAH
The Florsheim
SHOE

SAN FRANCISCO'S CENTURY OF STREET CARS

FRED A. STINDT

SAN FRANCISCO'S CENTURY OF STREET CARS

Library of Congress Catalog Card No. 90-90201

ISBN 0-9615465-1-4

Published by

Fred A. Stindt

3363 Riviera West Drive
Kelseyville, California 95451

FIRST PRINTING — OCTOBER 1990

ENDSHEETS

FRONT — In the heyday of the 1920's with hundreds of street cars rolling into downtown, Market Street is a busy thoroughfare as pedestrians alight and scurry to their destinations. *Ted Wurm Collection.*

BACK — Muni Light Rail Vehicle (LRV) #1325 at the Van Ness subway station is one of a fleet of 128 cars in subway service. The five underground lines transport over 130,000 passengers each working day. *Joshua Rotsten (SFPUC) photo.*

FRONTSPIECE

At 5:10 p.m., March 20, 1940, it was the usual string of street cars to handle the homebound commuter rush. Scene at Market, Geary and Kearny with the Palace Hotel in the background. *Carmen Magana (SFPUC), Muni Collection.*

TABLE OF CONTENTS

TO
MY WIFE
JANE
whose encouragement, helpful assistance and sincere interest has greatly inspired me in the publication of this book.

PREFACE

As San Francisco approaches a century of electric street cars in 1992; the past 100 years has seen the greatest assortment of electric transit vehicles that ever rode the flanged wheel on fixed rail. In the years gone by, many cities in the United States have completely abandoned the street car in favor of buses; electric, gas or diesel, but San Francisco has retained its rail transit and has seen first hand, the evolution of the street car from the single truck variety of the early days to the modern sleek streamline Light Rail Vehicle (LRV) in service today. They were all there in various sizes and shapes — over 2,000 of them, that at one time or other, plied the streets in the City by the Bay. This book features these cars and gives a concise history of the main events as they occurred in the past century leading into the United Railroads, Market Street Railway and San Francisco's own Municipal Railway. Included in the story are the routes and the streets they traversed, generally after the disastrous earthquake and fire, April 18, 1906, along with a ready reference table as to when each line started (when known), and the last day of street car operation.

The first half of the book is devoted to the United Railroads/Market Street Railway, which had a total of 50 street car routes: 1-12; 14-36; 40-43, seven unnumbered lines and four, 32-35 that were only in operation during the 1915 Exposition and then assigned to other unnumbered established lines. The remainder of the book is on the Municipal Railway, which had 17 routes: "A" to "O," which included two different "J" lines, and one short-lived number route, "32" during the year 1948. Five of these routes remain today, J-K-L-M and N. A new line to be known as the "F" line for service on Market Street from Castro, to Embarcadero and the Fisherman's Wharf area is scheduled to partially begin in 1993.

Included with the interesting history is a wealth of beautiful sharp clear photographs obtained from the best of transit historians and photographers along with several from the files of the San Francisco Municipal Railway (San Francisco Public Utilities Commission), credited for brevity, Muni collection or Muni photo. All photos are captioned as to location and date if known.

Every effort has been made to ensure accuracy, but mistakes or typographical errors may occur. If the reader has reason to believe there is an error in the text or caption or in the dates quoted, and has proof, the author would sincerely appreciate receiving the information.

The book is strictly on electric street cars. Cable cars, trolly coaches and motor buses are not included in this treatise.

Fred A. Stindt

Kelseyville, California
July, 1990

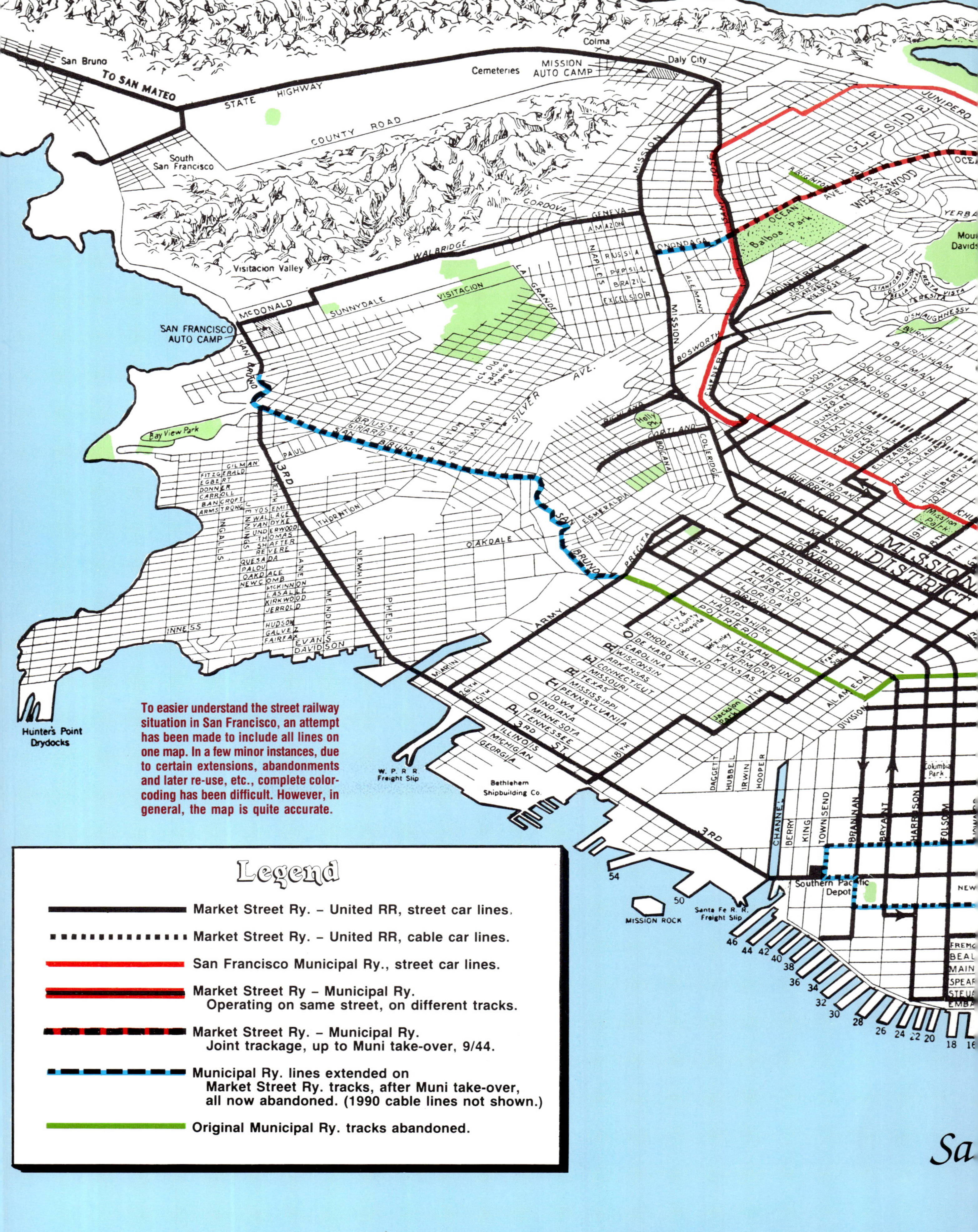

To easier understand the street railway situation in San Francisco, an attempt has been made to include all lines on one map. In a few minor instances, due to certain extensions, abandonments and later re-use, etc., complete color-coding has been difficult. However, in general, the map is quite accurate.
Legend
Market Street Ry. – United RR, street car lines.
Market Street Ry. – United RR, cable car lines.
San Francisco Municipal Ry., street car lines.
Market Street Ry – Municipal Ry. Operating on same street, on different tracks.
Market Street Ry. – Municipal Ry. Joint trackage, up to Muni take-over, 9/44.
Municipal Ry. lines extended on Market Street Ry. tracks, after Muni take-over, all now abandoned. (1990 cable lines not shown.)
Original Municipal Ry. tracks abandoned.
San Bruno
TO SAN MATEO
STATE HIGHWAY
COUNTY ROAD
South San Francisco
Colma
Daly City
Cemeteries
MISSION AUTO CAMP
Visitacion Valley
SAN FRANCISCO AUTO CAMP
Bay View Park
Hunter's Point Drydocks
INGLESIDE
Balboa Park
MISSION DISTRICT
W. P. R. R. Freight Slip
Bethlehem Shipbuilding Co.
MISSION ROCK
Santa Fe R. R. Freight Slip
Southern Pacific Depot
Columbia Park
Jackson Park
Mission Park
Garfield Sq.
Holly Pk.
City & County Hospital
Lick Old Ladies Home
POTRERO
Sa

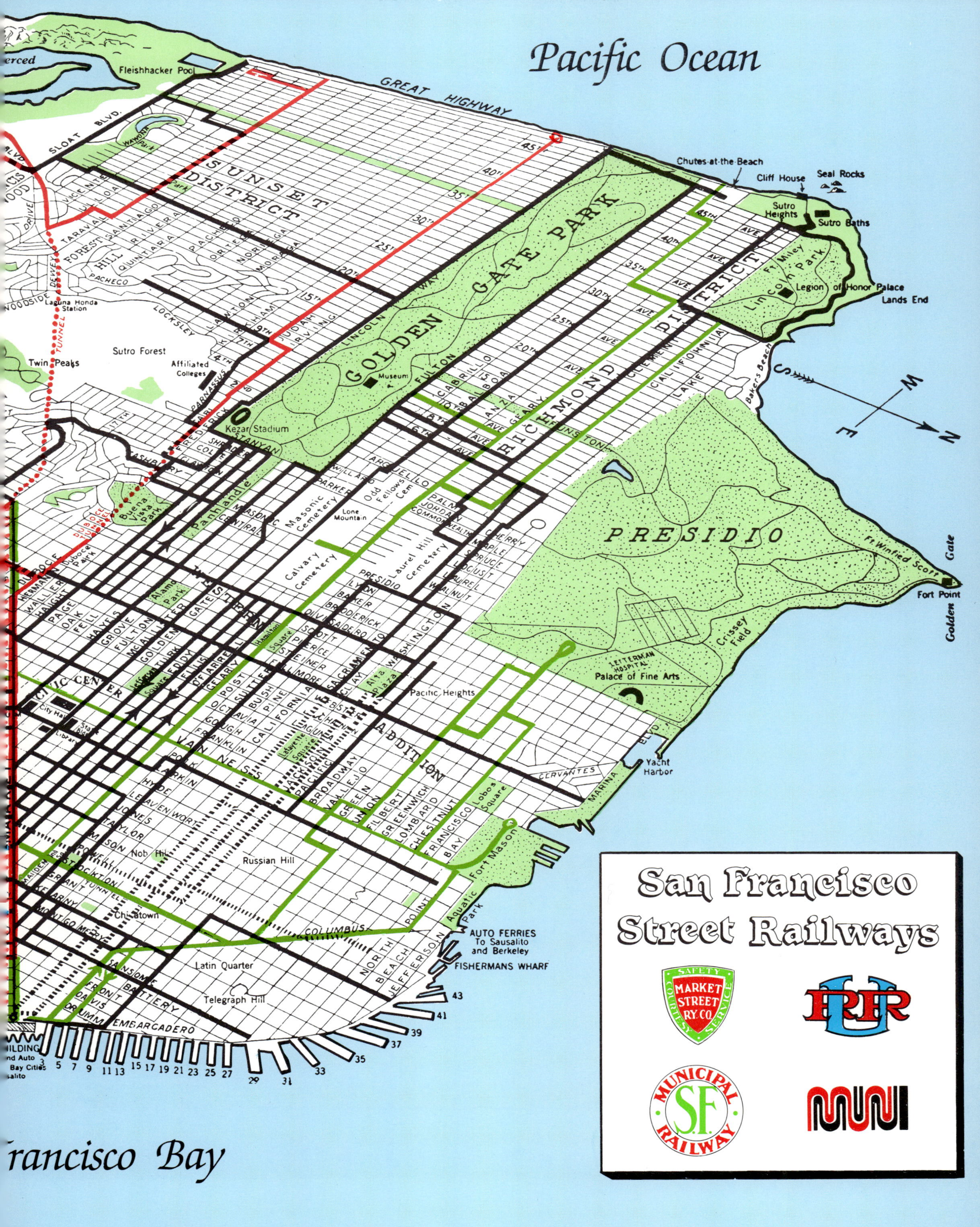
Pacific Ocean
Francisco Bay
San Francisco
Street Railways
MARKET STREET RY. CO.
SAFETY COURTESY SERVICE
MUNICIPAL S.F. RAILWAY
GOLDEN GATE PARK
SUNSET DISTRICT
RICHMOND DISTRICT
PRESIDIO
WESTERN ADDITION
GREAT HIGHWAY
Fleishhacker Pool
Chutes-at-the-Beach
Cliff House
Seal Rocks
Sutro Heights
Sutro Baths
Lincoln Park
Legion of Honor Palace
Lands End
Bakers Beach
Fort Point
Golden Gate
Palace of Fine Arts
Crissey Field
Yacht Harbor
Pacific Heights
Russian Hill
Nob Hill
Chinatown
Latin Quarter
Telegraph Hill
FISHERMANS WHARF
AUTO FERRIES To Sausalito and Berkeley
Aquatic Park
Fort Mason
Sutro Forest
Twin Peaks
Affiliated Colleges
Kezar Stadium
Museum
Laguna Honda Station
TWIN PEAKS TUNNEL
Buena Vista Park
Alamo Park
Lone Mountain
Masonic Cemetery
Odd Fellows Cem.
Calvary Cemetery
Laurel Hill Cemetery
Alta Plaza
Lafayette Square
Hamilton Square
City Hall
EMBARCADERO
COLUMBUS

Platform men pose for picture at outer terminal of #26 line at San Jose Ave. and Mission St., Daly City, circa 1910.
Tom Gray collection.

ACKNOWLEDGMENTS

To produce a book of this magnitude which contains so much historical data and photographs required the help of many. My interest and accumulation of material has been in progress for many years. I can recall my first visit with the dean of San Francisco's street car knowledge, the late Charles Smallwood over fifty years ago. Meeting at his home on 2nd Avenue, we traded negatives, photographs and informative data and later when he moved to 40th Avenue, the enjoyable get-togethers continued in my constant quest for historical information. There were also other San Francisco street car enthusiasts; Ted Wurm who resided on McAllister Street, later Monte Vista Avenue, Oakland; Bert Ward on 3rd Avenue later Eugene, Oregon; Tom Gray, Madrid Street later Burlingame (who printed several hundred quality photos for this book), and Douglas Richter 6th Avenue later San Bruno. The many visits to these fine gentlemen, who all became good friends, produced a wealth of data and photos of San Francisco street cars. In later years there were others who graciously opened up their files and made available material and photographs; Richard Schlaich, Philip Hoffman, Will Whittaker, Arthur Lloyd, Warren Miller, Jerry Graham, Bob Stein, Harre Demoro, Jeft Moreau, Fred Matthews, Jr., and the late Francis Guido. Each assisted me in my endeavor to gain as much knowledge as possible of the street cars that plied the streets in the City by the Golden Gate. Much historical material was gleaned from articles written by Wald Sievers for the Western Railroader magazine in 1965 and 1968. I wish to thank the Pacific Coast Chapter, Railway & Locomotive Historical Society, present publishers of the magazine for making this available to me and all other related items that appeared in the Western Railroader from time to time. Also, to Helen Guido for allowing me to use appropriate photos in the Guido collection. Considerable reference material was found in Charles Smallwood's book "White Front Cars of San Francisco;" Anthony Perles book "Peoples Railway;" and Anthony Perles/John Kane's book "Inside Muni (San Francisco Municipal Railway)". All three of these fine books were published by Interurban Press, Glendale, California. I also appreciate the help by the San Francisco library staff in assisting me in locating a number of transit articles in early day issues of the San Francisco Chronicle or Examiner.

Although I never met the late Henry Mentz, official photographer for United Railroads/Market Street Railway, I am indebted to him for the fine work he did in not only taking priceless photos, but preserving an accurate file. Many of these "gems" appear in this book. A big thank you, also, to Marshall Maxom, head of the San Francisco's Municipal Railway photo department until his retirement in 1979 and Carmen Magana, present head of Muni's photo lab. They have been most helpful and cooperative in my search of historical photos. My appreciation to Bruce Bernhard, manager of Muni's strategic planning for his generous cooperation in answering the many questions presented and Bob Caldwell, Community Affairs Department, for his help in supplying the latest maps and up-to-date information.

Typesetting was accomplished by Linnell Printing, Kelseyville, California. Many thanks to Mike Linnell and Kelly Sears, typesetter, in their dedication in producing the fine work as seen in the following pages. Thank you, also, to Helga Rose and Jane Stindt for their painstaking effort in proof reading the many pages of copy. Not to be forgotten is the superb presswork, which was accomplished by Tom Hoefer of Modesto Printing, Modesto, California. Lastly and certainly not least, a special thank you to Al Rose, long time friend and loyal supporter throughout the years, for his expertise in layout, printing and production of this fine book, San Francisco's Century of Street Cars.

HUMBOLDT BANK
HUMBOLDT BANK
COMMERCIAL TRUST
CALIFORNIA
States

CHAPTER I

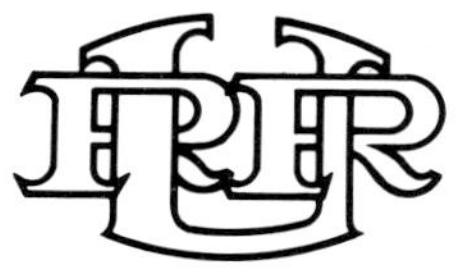

MARKET STREET RAILWAY CO. (UNITED RAILROADS)

In the morning edition of the San Francisco Examiner, April 27, 1892, buried in one of the inner pages, under the heading "To The Sepulchre By Wire" was the following excerpt; "At last San Francisco has an electric road. It took years of "promoting," tomes of campaign documents, many evidences of "inflooence," and a deal of quiet lobbying and loud cries of "boodle". Yesterday the road was finally opened with great joy and some wine for invited guests. The occasion was marked by triumph of energy and engineering over injunction suits, cantankerous property owners, shy legislators, elusive supervisors and wildly timerous stockholders. Today, the road will get down to their regular nickel-in-the-slot business," so read the article. The electric road known as the San Francisco & San Mateo Railway was a reality, the first electric street car operation in San Francisco. Ten month's earlier, July 29, 1891, a silver spike driving ceremony had taken place at high noon at a point on San Jose Avenue near Geothe Street (county line). President Behrend Joost of the railway company had the honor of driving the silver spike in place. Any reader know where this spike is today? The next century would see 67 street car lines established in San Francisco with over 2,000 street cars purchased or built in company shops to run over these lines at one time or other. The first trolley line ran from Steuart and Market Streets, to Harrison, 14th, Guerrero, 30th Street, Chenery, thence San Jose Avenue, Daly City (then known as Daly's Hill) and on to Holy Cross Cemetery. The operation went broke and a receiver was appointed in May, 1894. It was sold at a foreclosure sale, April 11, 1896. A year later the line was extended another mile to Baden.

The Metropolitan Railroad was the second electric trolley line in San Francisco, which went into operation, October 20, 1892. This operation began at Market and Eddy, out Eddy, to Hyde, thence O'Farrell, Scott, Fell, Baker, Page, Clayton, Waller to 9th Avenue and Lincoln Way, then known as "H" Street. A circuitous route that made one dizzy, but it was the company's intention to get as many streets in the franchise as possible.

On August 22, 1893, the Market Street Railway was organized with heavy backing from the Southern Pacific Railroad. The new company took over the Metropolitan Railroad and all cable lines in San Francisco with the exception of the SF&SM to Holy Cross and cable lines on Sutter, Geary, California and Union Streets. New electric street car lines started to blossom in all directions, with the exception of the main thoroughfare, Market Street, where an ordinance had been passed in 1891 prohibiting the installation of trolley wire on this main street. Too dangerous they said.

Meanwhile in the building surge, an argument heated up between Adolph Sutro and the Market Street Railway as the fares that would be charged in the establishment of a street car line to Sutro Baths adjacent to the Cliff House. With no agreement in sight, Adolph Sutro built his own electric line, the Sutter Street Railroad, from Presidio Avenue (then Central) and Sutter, to California, to Parker (then Williamson), to Euclid, Arguello (then First Ave.), Clement, 33rd Ave., Geary, 48th Ave., thence right-of-way to Sutro Baths terminal. The line was opened, February 1, 1896.

By the turn of the century there were at least 20 street car lines with over 400 street cars, mostly of the four wheel truck variety operating on those lines. Each line had its own cars assigned with a different paint decor for each line, i.e., Howard-Folsom line had a blue color, Ellis-O'Farrell, yellow, etc.

In 1902, a band of eastern capitalists formed the United Railroads. On March 8, 1902, they took over the Market Street Railway, Sutter Street Railroad and the San Francisco & San Mateo Railroad. Not included was the California Street Cable Railroad; Geary, Park & Ocean Railway and the Presidio & Ferries Railway. All in all the new ownership had 166.25 miles of electric traction and 414 street cars. The standard exterior color for all cars became red and cream.

While the routes were expanded and new lines built in San Francisco, the United Railroads extended the San Francisco and San Mateo Railway to San Mateo from

(Left) In front of the landmark Emporium Department store building, Market Street had four tracks for the many street cars that brought office workers and shoppers downtown. ***Tom Gray collection.***

(Above) Electric street car service in San Francisco began April 26, 1892. Motormen and conductors pose in uniforms of the day shortly after the official opening. ***Stindt collection.*** **(Left) The second street car line was the Metropolitan Railway which began October 20, 1892. Car had odd six-wheel Robinson Radial truck. The cumbersome arrangement did not last long and was replaced with a standard four-wheel truck.** ***Tom Gray collection.***

(Left) Another new electric street car line was Sutro Railroad built by Adolph Sutro. When an agreement could not be reached with the old Market Street Railway as to fares to be charged to his amusement park at Sutro Baths near the famed Cliff House at Seal Rocks, Sutro built his own line. Car #39 poses outside the large car barn at 33rd and Clement. ***Smallwood collection.*** **(Below) Built as an open car for the Metropolitan Railway in 1893 and numbered 37. It was rebuilt by the Market Street Railway in 1895 as a California type car and given #1092 with assignment to the Howard Street line.** ***Gilbert Kneiss collection.***

(Top) One of the early double truck cars, #1008, on the original Market Street Railway's Mission Street line. Painted green and cream, the photo was taken in mid-1890's. The early cars had no front or rear windows. Note platform men heavily clothed for the cold days that can prevail in San Francisco. *Gilbert Kneiss collection.* (Center) By 1900 front and rear windows were installed on all cars. Car #444 in yellow hue is assigned to the Ellis-O'Farrell line. *L.B. Slevin collection.* (Below) Single truck car #653 poses for official United Railroads photo in the early 1910's. This car was assigned to the Fillmore counter balance system in 1915 and rebuilt with a hooking device and with electric connections so it could run in multiple units. The car came to an end when it ran away on the Fillmore hill, jumped the track and crashed into a pole, November 16, 1921. The cost of repair was too great, so car was scrapped. *United Railroads.*

(Above) Built by the St. Louis Car Company in 1903-05. Car #1316 as shown in this photo was built with wire mesh along outside seats as a safety factor. The 125 cars in this series were completely rebuilt into California type Pay As You Enter cars in 1912-1913. *Bob Stein collection.*

(Below) The finest street cars were twenty purchased from Laelede Car Company in 1903. Briefly assigned to the San Mateo line, they were replaced by the "Big Subs" in 1906, and assigned to local Mission Street routes. When the "Big Subs" were phased out in 1923, the Laelede cars returned to the Peninsula line. Photo shows car #1231 under United Railroads. *United Railroads.*

Holy Cross via private right-of-way and along city streets in Burlingame and San Mateo to the downtown Southern Pacific station in San Mateo. The old line to the east from Holy Cross to Baden, approximately one mile, was declared surplus and turned over to a newly formed subsidiary; South San Francisco Railroad and Power Company formed by the San Francisco Land and Improvement Company to build a line to Point San Bruno on San Francisco Bay to open up residential and industrial areas. This line went across the new Bayshore Southern Pacific Railroad cut-off at Grand Avenue and continued to the Western Meat Company plant. Total length 3.0 miles. The underpass at Holy Cross was a problem, as each winter it filled with water putting the line out of service for weeks at a time. On June 18, 1916, the connection for the #40 San Mateo line was changed to Leipsic Junction (Baden), located at the western end of Grand Ave. This ended the Holy Cross underpass problems with one mile abandoned.

Built before the turn-of-the-century Sutro Baths became one of the most popular recreational spots in San Francisco. The #2 line had its terminus in the building shown at the upper right. Cars ran every five minutes during the Sunday summer peak periods to downtown and the Ferry Loop. ***Unknown collection.***

Car #1401 at Ellis and Taylor heading to 19th and H Street (now Lincoln Way) in the year 1905. These cars #1300-1424 arrived from the builder St. Louis Car Co., in 1903-1905 with closed center section and open ends. Note open ends have a wire mesh for protection of the patrons. ***Gilbert Kneiss collection.***

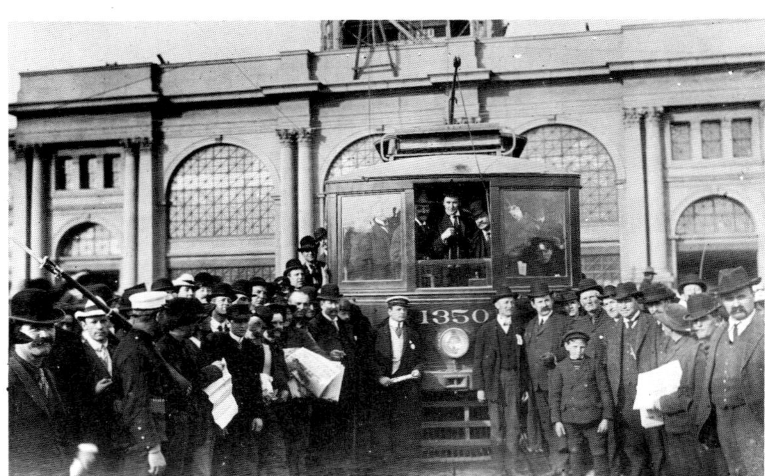

(Above) Note total devistation of downtown San Francisco as wrought by the earthquake and resulting fire, April 18, 1906. The photo was taken from the top of the Ferry Building a week later. Market Street is at the left where street cars will replace the ruined cable car system in less than a month. (Center) The first electric street car to officially operate on Market Street. Aboard were Mayor Schmitz and many dignitaries. An enthusiastic crowd gathered at the Ferry Building to be on hand for the inaugural run with car #1350, with its new green paint decor, May 2, 1906. *United Railroads.* (Below) Car #1382 rolls along Mission Street at 7th with the main Post Office on left, in the Fall of 1906. Note devastation remaining from earthquake and fire. *Tom Gray collection.*

(Left) Destined for the Chicago Railways an order of 50 street cars was diverted to San Francisco when the city was in dire need following the earthquake destruction in April, 1906. Car #1503 shown not long after its arrival. These cars became known as the "Chicago cars". ***Tom Gray collection.*** **(Below) With cable mechanism removed, cable car #247 of the former Hayes cable line, is used as a trailer with street car #1551 on the #9 Valencia line to assist with peak periods in 1908. The arrangement was short-lived.** ***Smallwood collection.***

With a growing street car system some of the original cars became obsolete. United Railroads between 1903 and 1905 purchased 146 large double truck street cars. Twenty, a solid interurban type, were obtained from Laclede Car Company, given numbers 1225-1244 and placed on the San Mateo line. They were the first street cars in San Francisco equipped with air brakes. Of the remaining 126 new cars, 125 came from the St. Louis Car Company in three groups numbered 1300-1349, 1350-1374, 1375-1424. One other 2nd #1350 was purchased from the Pressed Steel Car Company.

Then came the earthquake and resulting fire, April 18, 1906. The damage was astronomical with 497 blocks covering five square miles destroyed. The five heavy travelled Market Street cable lines (McAllister, Hayes, Haight, Valencia and Castro) with their powerhouses and winding machinery were in shambles. Surprisingly, only six street cars were destroyed by the raging inferno. A permit was obtained quickly from the city to allow trolley wire on Market Street for take over by electric street cars of the former cable lines.

With clean up and reconstruction going on 24 hours of the day Market Street was ready for the first electric street car operation on May 6, 1906, to replace the destroyed cable car lines. Chosen for the event was street car #1350. With Mayor Eugene Schmitz, mayor of San Francisco at the controls, the car moved slowly along the famous street for the several blocks in operation amidst thousands of cheering workers who were still busy with clean up and rebuilding. Electric traction had come to Market Street along with a new exterior paint decor. Henceforth all cars would be painted Pullman green with yellow lettering.

Learning that 50 street cars built by the American Car Company were ready for delivery to the Chicago City Railway, an urgent appeal was made for these cars. Sympathetic officials of the Chicago company diverted the order to San Francisco. They were given numbers 1500-1549 and became known as the "Chicago Cars". For years they were mainly assigned to the #5 McAllister and #21 Hayes lines working out of the McAllister car barn.

The need for additional cars was great, so president Patrick Calhoun scoured the East to see what he could find. At the St. Louis Car Company plant he found twelve suburban motor cars and four trailers that had been built for the Philadelphia and Western Railway, but that company had gone broke. They were just the ticket for the San Mateo line, so they were purchased on the spot. Transported to San Francisco, the motor cars were soon rolling on the San Mateo line replacing the short-lived 1225 class, which were reassigned to Mission Street local routes. The four trailers were sold to Northern Electric Railway, who converted them to motor units. (They became part of the Sacramento Northern in later years). The large cars became known as "Big

"Big Sub" #8 poses for a company photo at the Geneva car barn, April 4, 1916. *United Railroads.*

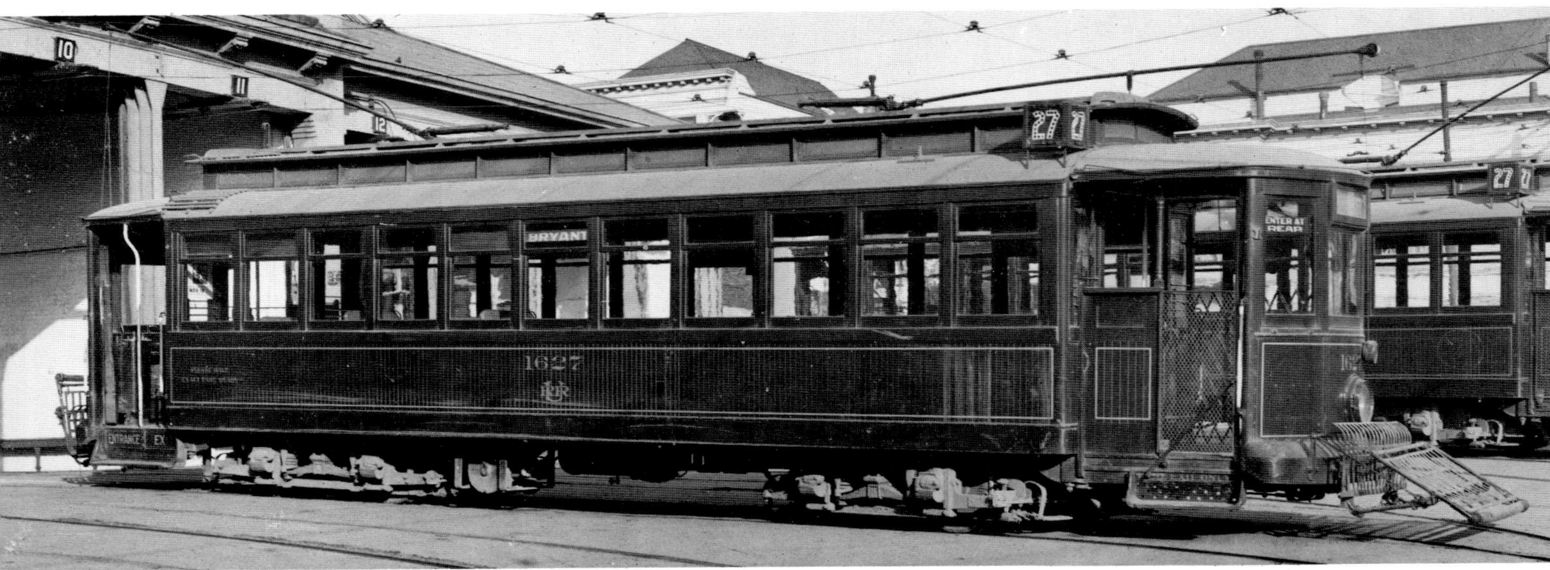

(Above) The largest street car order in San Francisco was placed in 1907; 200 street cars from the St. Louis Car Company. Fenders and route boxes applied the following year as shown by the appearance of Car #1627 at the 24th and Utah car barn. (Left) Car #1400 poses for a sharp clear photo near Turk and Fillmore car barn, February 27, 1917. Ready for the #22 line run, the car was rebuilt at Elkton Shops in 1913 to a PAYE California type car. *Both photos United Railroads, Richard Schliach collection.*

Car second #1350, built by St. Louis Car Co. in 1904 poses for a photo at 24th and Utah in the 1920's. First #1350 (of which no photo exists) built by the Press Steel Co. in 1903, took on the number 1391 in 1910 after being out of service for modifications practically from its delivery date. ***Tom Gray collection.***

Subs''. Unfortunately they were heavy power users, so in 1923 they were placed in storage and offered for sale. The 1225 class went back to the San Mateo service. After ten years in storage and no takers, the ''Big Subs'' were scrapped. While in the East president Calhoun also placed the largest order ever with the St. Louis Car Company; 200 street cars to be built along the lines of the Chicago cars. They were given numbers 1550-1749.

Sutter Street was also ready for electric street cars. The operation commenced on June 4, 1906. As they came into Market Street they glided along newly installed tracks alongside the center tracks from Sutter Street to the Ferry Loop. It was the beginning of four tracks on the thoroughfare that in a few years would see four tracks along its entire length. However, a franchise dispute arose with the city, which resulted in horse car substitution on Market Street effective, June 1, 1908. In other words Sutter Street car patrons had to transfer to a horse car to continue on to the Ferry Loop. This operation went on for five long years until the Municipal Railway wanted outer tracks for their new Geary Street lines to the Ferry Loop. A horse car mixed into the operation would not lend to any scheduling, so the Board of Supervisors quickly passed an ordinance forbidding horse car lines anywhere in the city effective, June 2, 1913. The following day, the horse car ran on its last trip with Mayor ''Sunny'' Jim Rolph, Patrick Calhoun, president of United Railroads, and other dignitaries aboard Trailer #45 (a mate #54 is on display at the Cable Car Museum, San Francisco). Of interesting note, each morning the horse car had to be towed by street car from its barn on Pacific Avenue to Sutter and Market to start its run. At night it was towed back. Truly, it was the end of the horse car era.

Of serious concern, which placed a cap on future expansion of United Railroads was the adoption of a charter for the City and County of San Francisco that was voted and placed in effect, January 8, 1900. It read ''It is the purpose and intention of the City and County of San Francisco that public utilities shall be gradually acquired and ultimately owned by San Francisco.'' An amendment to this charter occurred two years later by reducing franchise grants to 25 years. In 1910, another amendment clouded the picture even more, as it gave the city the right to purchase any line or lines provided by future franchises. There was little expansion after that date by United Railroads, such expansion was left to the newly established Municipal Railway, which started in 1912. It was of great concern to the private company.

The year 1908 saw the introduction of eclipse fenders (commonly known as ''cow catchers'') installed on street cars. Also, it was the beginning of route numbers placed on boxes on the roof at each end of the car.

(Above) Double truck car #1007 on the Folsom Street line heading for Precita Avenue at York, September 18, 1914. ***Tom Gray collection.*** **(Center) Single truck car #657 on the 3rd and Harrison-Park line, which would become the #33 line after 1915.** ***Bert Ward collection.*** **(Bottom) The only single truck street car saved from the Market Street or United Railroads that plied the streets of San Francisco at one time or other. Built in 1895, it became sand car #0601 under United Railroads. Municipal Railway restored the car, #578, to its former yellow livery elegance in 1956, as shown in this photo taken at the Geneva Car barn. Today the historic car is part of the Festival fleet and is used for historic occasions.** ***Stindt photo.***

By 1911 many of the turn-of-the-century cars were becoming obsolete and were phased out and scrapped. This included an assortment of single truck cars in the 500 to 1100 series. Twenty-nine were sold to Presidio and Ferries Railway and many others converted into service cars. Sixty-two that were in the best condition were overhauled and placed in the 601-662 series for further use on small lines. The rest were junked. Most of the double truck cars in the 600, 700, 900, 1000 and 1100 series were also sent to the scrap yard. However, many were stripped for parts and motors that were used in reconditioning older cars that were retained or for use on cars being built at Elkton shops.

Up to 1911, passengers could board a street car, sit down and the conductor would come through, collect the fare and ring it up on the register. United Railroads introduced the **P**ay **A**s **Y**ou **E**nter system. Passengers would board at the rear of the car, pay the fare before going to their seat. This proved more convenient and certainly more economical, so all cars were quickly converted to the new fare collecting method.

Car #134 built by Jewett Car Company in 1911 poses for a photograph outside the Haight Street car barn, November 27, 1914. *United Railroads.*

THE UNITED RAILROADS OF SAN FRANCISCO

EARNESTLY REQUESTS

THE PUBLIC TO CO-OPERATE IN FACILITATING TRANSPORTATION IN THE USE OF

Pay-As-You-Enter Cars

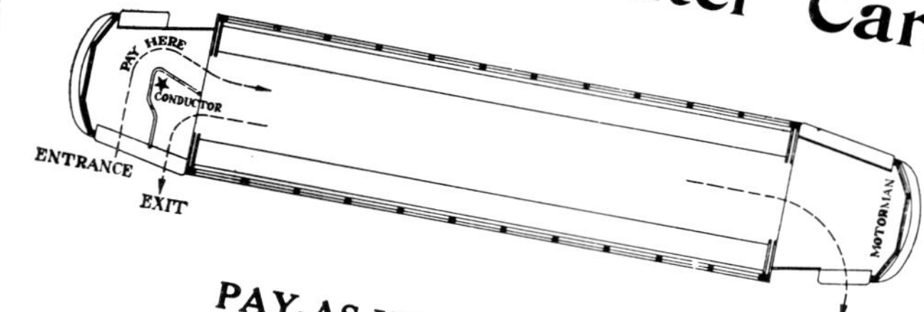

PAY-AS-YOU-ENTER CAR

PLEASE HAVE YOUR FARE RE
BEFORE BOARDING THIS CA

DISTINCTIVE FEATURES OF THE

PAY-AS-YOU-ENTER CAR

PASSENGER BOARDING CAR

PASSENGER LEAVING CAR

THE **PAY-AS-YOU-ENTER CAR** introduces system in place of confusion, adding greatly to the safety, comfort and satisfaction of passengers, and to the rapidity of service.

In order that the operation of the **PAY-AS-YOU-ENTER CAR** may be successful, and that the benefits to passengers be fully realized, the public is respectfully requested to assist the company by observing the following regulations.

PRINCIPLES OF OPERATING P-A-Y-E CARS

Board car only at rear platform by step marked "ENTRANCE."
Conductor will always be on rear platform to insure safety of passengers.
Passengers will not be annoyed by conductor passing through car.
Congestion on rear platform will be eliminated and passageway will always be clear.
HAVE EXACT CASH FARE, TRANSFER OR TICKET READY BEFORE BOARDING CAR, pay to conductor on rear platform and pass inside at once.
Passengers not having exact fare will please step to rear of platform until those having exact fare have passed into car.
Have transfer unfolded when giving to conductor.
Ask for transfer, if desired, when paying fare.
Passengers desiring information, should step to extreme rear of platform.
Conductors are not required to change coin or bills of larger denomination than $5.00.
Passengers will leave car by front exit, getting off at step marked "EXIT."
When necessary, leave car by rear exit, getting off at step marked "EXIT."
No baggage, bundles or baby carriages will be permitted on rear platform. No dogs or large bundles will be permitted on cars.
Electric signal push buttons are located between all windows. Press button as signal for car to stop.
Signal for car to stop one-half block from corner.
On account of city ordinances, it will be impossible to permit smoking on any part of these cars.

CHAS. N. BLACK
Vice-Pres't and Gen'l M'g'r.

The Pay As You Enter system was inaugurated in 1911 and proved highly popular from the start. These flyers explained the new system to street car patrons. *Stindt collection.*

(Above) Designed by United Railroads chief draftsman, W.D. Farlow, this car known as the California type became the prototype of hundreds of electric street cars that were built in San Francisco in the next two decades. The first in an order of 65, #201, poses for a company photo at the Point Lobos terminal of the #1 line shortly after received from the builder, the American Car Company, September 18, 1913. *Bob Stein collection.* (Right) The terminus for the scenic #1 Land's End line was the Point Lobos station at 48th Avenue. It was built by the steam operated Ferries and Cliff House Railroad in 1887. Market Street Railway took over this line, October 14, 1894. Rebuilt for electric operation. It became the #1 line. Later tracks were curved into the #2 line at 48th Avenue, so the #1 cars could run to Sutro Baths on Sundays and holidays. *Tom Gray collection.*

Because of the crowded conditions at the base of the Ferry Building, the Mission, Howard and Folsom car line terminous was moved to the center of Embarcadero. Relaying of tracks scene, December 8 , 1912. *Richard Schlaich collection.*

MARKET STREET RY CO.
CHUTES

Car #1614 ready for its run on the #9 Valencia line. Note open section in front, which was adapted on about half of this type of car between 1916-1918. By the late 1920's they were all enclosed again. ***United Railroads.***

(Previous page)
(Top) At the turn of the century single truck car #770 stops for a company photo half way up Fillmore Hill near Vallejo. Note hooking device to counter balance in front. Cars 751-770 were assigned to this line, which became known as the #22 line. ***Gilbert Kneiss collection.*** **(Center) Hook tender is applying hooking device on car #624 prior to ascending hill between Green and Broadway on Fillmore.** ***Guido collection.*** **(Bottom) To handle the 1915 Panama Pacific Golden Gate Exposition, fourteen single truck cars were rebuilt so they could operate multiple on the Fillmore Street Hill.** ***United Railroads.***

Also, in 1911 an order for 80 more street cars were given to the Jewett Car Company. When they arrived it was found they had no compartments for a smoking section and uncomfortable longitudinal rattan seats. Hardly a public relations item and the riding public gave them a poor rating. First they were placed on the Sutter lines and then the three Haight Street lines became their home. In 1927, the cars received deep leather cushion cross seats throughout, which included a smoking section. Needless to say, the cars jumped to first place in the eyes of the public for a comfortable ride.

An important step in street car design took place in 1913. Designed by W.B. Farlow, head draftsman for United Railroads, this type of car became the prototype of all future San Francisco street cars for the next several decades, even for those ordered by the Municipal Railway in later years. Sixty-five of these successful cars with their easy boarding made possible by large drop platforms, were ordered from the American Car Company, St. Louis, and delivered to San Francisco in the year 1913. They followed the California type design of open ends and closed center section. In the 1920's the cars were enclosed. The cars assigned to the Sutter 1-2-3 lines remained there for much of their life. When Muni took over in 1944, to avoid a number conflict many were renumbered into the 600 series (see roster section). A good number saw service on Muni's Geary lines.

San Francisco was selected as the site of the Panama-Pacific Exposition to be held in 1915. The new Municipal Railway laid much new trackage and was a very competing source for the crowds that came to visit

ENTRANCE EXIT 
ALAMEDA
Coca-Cola
LINCOLN HOTEL
CIGARS
POOL
DRINKS

the spectacle. The Exposition was bounded by Van Ness Avenue to the Presidio and Chestnut Street to the bay. United Railroads established an Exposition Terminal by installing a loop in the Polk, Francisco, Van Ness area served by the #19 line. In addition four new temporary lines were placed into service to this terminal.

#32 Southern Pacific Depot-Exposition. S.P. Depot, Townsend, 4th, Ellis, Hyde, O'Farrell, Polk to Terminal.
#33 Mission-Exposition. 29th and Mission, on Mission to 9th, Larkin, Post, Polk to Terminal.
#34 Sutter-Exposition. Ferry via Market, Sutter, Polk to Terminal.
#35 Haight-Exposition. Carl and Stanyan, on Carl to Clayton, Frederick, Masonic, Page, (return via Oak) Fillmore to Broadway. This line lasted less than two months.

After the Exposition was over these four route numbers were assigned to other lines. On the Fillmore counterbalance, which served the Fair directly, fourteen single truck cars were rebuilt so they could operate in multiple units.

One of the smaller lines was destined to cause havoc with the entire future of United Railroads. This was the Visitacion Valley line, which operated from Geneva and Mission to the County Road at Sunnyvale (Six Mile House). Total 2.5 miles and opened October 25, 1909 to develop a residential area. The disaster took place during World War I. Patronage in the morning and evening rush hours was heavy with workers heading for shipyards building ships for the war effort, but otherwise the loads were scant. For that reason, United Railroads took three of the 1001-1025 series cars and converted them into one-man operation; 1022, 1023 and 1024. The one man service started in 1914. On that fateful morning, July 12, 1918, car #1022 loaded with almost 100 passengers took off from the Mission Terminal and headed downhill. The car lost its air and consequently had no brakes. With the rush of speed it could not make the turn at the foot of the grade when turning into Schwerin Street from Walbridge and crashed over on its side. Eight were killed and 70 injured. While United immediately withdrew one-man cars, San Francisco enacted an ordinance forbidding one-man car operation. A few other short lines, such as Parkside, Bosworth and Divisadero Extension also had been converted to one-man operation by conversion of several single truck cars; 601-605, 613-616. With two men back on the cars, the conductor stood alongside the motorman on these cars to collect fares.

United Railroads was embroiled in two disruptive labor disputes in 1907 and 1917, which did not help patronage nor their public image. Also, to further hinder their struggle for survival, unregulated jitney bus service started in 1915 along profitable lines, such as Mission Street. Also, in 1914, the City cancelled on September 5th, the franchise on California Street from 6th to 33rd Avenue to make way for Municipal Railway's "C" line. United then had to shift its #1 line by turning at 6th Avenue for one block to Clement thence to 33rd Avenue and resume private-right-of-way to Point Lobos Station. The Muni's "C" line became a competitor to both the #1 and #2 lines.

By 1921 United Railroads was on the "ropes". On April 1, a newly formed Market Street Railway took over and a new management team installed. The first order of the day was to improve the public image, which had hit rock bottom. Beginning in 1920 and continuing through 1933, an ambitious program of building new street cars took place. This was the 266-305 and 778-994 group, a total of 257 cars. Elkton shops turned out approximately two a month. The cars were known as

(Right) Built at Elkton Shops and ready for service May 6, 1924 is car #800. In its green paint and yellow lettering this car is assigned to the #22 line. ***Tom Gray collection.***

(Previous page)
(Top) Market Street at Third, February 14, 1917. Among the "flivers" is rebuilt "Chicago" car #1508. ***Ted Wurm collection.*** **(Bottom) Market at Spear, June 23, 1921. Note tower on the corner, which shunts street cars to outer track to Ferry Loop. Southern Pacfic building in background.** ***Ted Wurm collection.***

Old Mission
Brunswick
CURTAINS
FACTORY PRICES
PACIFIC HOTEL
Worn the World Over
Boston Garter
Velvet Grip
Camel
50 Good Cigarettes 10¢
GENUINE
"BULL" DURHAM
TOBACCO
GHIRARDELLI'S COCOA & GROUND CHOCOLATE

(Above) When this photo was taken at the Mission-Howard Terminal, a total of eight lines used this terminus, as can be attested by the information boards posted. The area was just south of the Market Street Ferry Loop. The Pacific Hotel offered attractive rates of 50 cnts to $1.50 per day. ***Muni photo.***

(Previous page)
(Upper) Looking south from the Ferry Building; Ferry Loop and Mission-Howard terminal in the 1920's. Today (1990) the scene is a drastic change-looking at a two-deck unattractive freeway. (Lower) During the heyday of the 1920's, the Ferry Building, built in 1896, was the second busiest passenger terminal in the world, behind Charing Cross in London. Note crowds walking on the overpass from the second floor of the Ferry Building across the Embaradero at 8:45 a.m. ***Both Mike McGarvey collection.***

"California Comfort Cars". Six of the Fillmore counterbalance cars were extensively rebuilt 621-625, 627. By 1927, leather cushion comfy-cozy seats were installed in many of the older cars, such as the Jewetts in the 101-180 series replacing wooden or rattan seats. Many of the earlier models constructed had trucks and motors from scrapped 1300-1400 series cars and in the 1930 models some had trucks from the 1600 class that were being phased out at the time.

To further improve the image, the railway introduced the California blue and gold street car on June 9, 1925, to commemorate California's Diamond Jubilee. Instead of having the next number in new construction sequence #299, the car emerged as #2001. The car with its bright yellow paint scheme and blue trim and lettering was given a great deal of publicity. As street cars go, it was a beautiful looking car. It won immediate public favor. Fourteen cars received this treatment. Another ten were scheduled, but control of the Market Street Railway was taken over by The Standard Power and Light Corporation, a subsidiary of Standard Gas and Electric Company in 1925. At the same time Byllesby Engineering and Management Corporation took over the management of the trolley system.

While the colorful blue and gold cars were pleasing to the citizens of San Francisco, Byllesby had other ideas. On January 13, 1926, car #809 came out of the Elkton Shops with a gleaming white front, red front window sash trim, roof border and buffer. At night it was brightly illuminated, a safety feature, to cut down

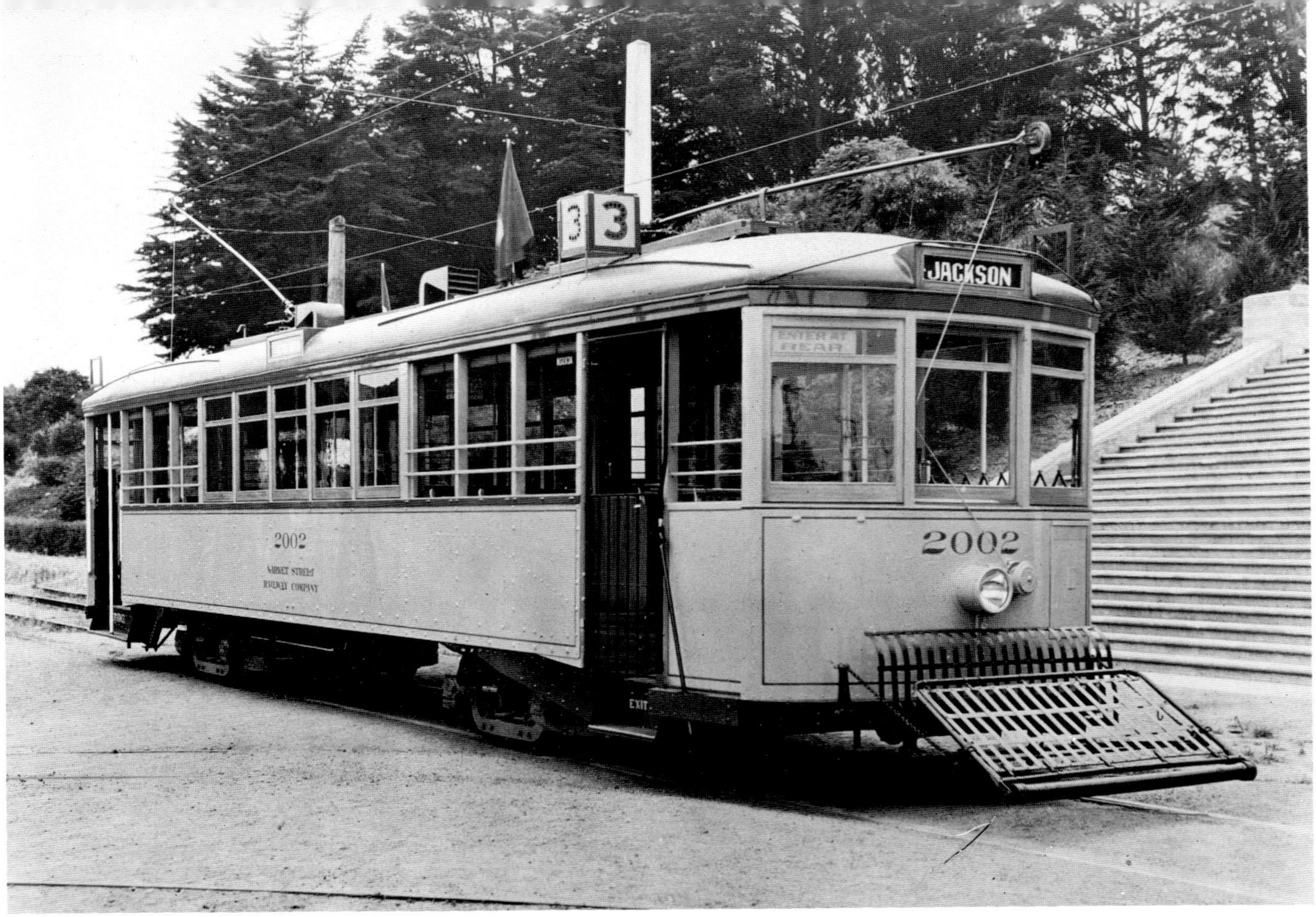

(Above) To commemorate California's Golden Jubilee, the Market Street Railway outshopped 14 street cars at their Elkton Shops painted blue and gold (yellow). The attractive decor lasted only a few months, as a new paint style known as the "White Front" with green sides took its place. #2001-2014 were renumbered into their original planned sequence; #299-305 and #837-843. ***Richard Schlaich collection.*** **(Center) Car #271, built by Elkton Shops in 1920 sports the new White Front color scheme in the year 1925. Note forward section open but rear section has been closed in.** ***Tom Gray collection.*** **(Bottom) Car #762 on the #33 line has completed the switchback from Market Street and is heading up Clayton Street to its destination at Golden Gate Park in 1930. Note Ford "fliver" in the foreground, in U.S. Mail service.** ***Bert Ward collection.***

In appreciation of the voters of San Francisco okaying a blanket 25 year operating permit for all lines, the Market Street Railway constructed a new line out Balboa to 30th Avenue. The line was opened May 14, 1932 with much fanfare as can be seen in the photo, with high-speed cars assigned it was popular from the start. *Smallwood collection.*

accidents. It was a highly successful innovation, so much so, that a patent was obtained in February, 1927. All street cars received the white front as fast as they could paint them. The colorful blue and gold cars disappeared overnight and were renumbered into their original planned sequence #299-305 and #837-843 with green sides and the new white fronts.

Mother nature had a hand in causing another blow to the well-being of the trolley system when on February 7, 1925, a huge slide occurred on the Land's End scenic #1 line overlooking the Pacific Ocean. It was deemed too expensive to repair so the entire section was abandoned. Henceforth the #1 line would terminate at 33rd and Clement. However, when the ship COOS BAY slammed on the rocks at China Beach near Mile Rock, October 22, 1927, one track to Land's end was reactivated for rescue efforts by breach buoys.

The year 1929 saw many franchises expire, some of the most heavy used street car lines included. With a better public image established, the voters of San Francisco gave approval for the Market Street Railway to turn in its remaining franchises to the City and County of San Francisco and in turn receive a blanket 25 year operating permit for all lines. With that the Market Street Railway went about to fulfill some of its campaign promises by constructing a new line out Balboa Street to 30th Avenue. It was opened with much fanfare on May 14, 1932. Given the route number 31, it was popular from the start with the new high-speed 900 series cars assigned.

The beginning of the 1930 decade saw the highest number of street car lines attained by the Market Street Railway. To service the many cars the transit system had a total of ten car barns. They were as follows, with the routes shown of the street cars they serviced and maintained:

Geneva (Geneva at San Jose Ave.)	10, 12, 18, 26, 40, So. San Francisco & Visitacion Valley lines.
28th & Valencia	8-9-14
29th & Mission	11-23-24, Bosworth
Third Street (3rd at 23rd Streets)	15-16-28-29-30-41-42-43, 1st & 5th line.
24th & Utah	19-25-27-34-35-36, 10th & Montgomery
Fillmore (Fillmore at Turk)	4-22-31, Fillmore Hill, Divisadero Extension
Oak & Broderick	6-20-32, Parkside
Haight Street (near Stanyan)	7-17-33
McAllister (at Central)	5-21
Sutro (Clement & 32nd)	1-2-3-4

A storage yard area known as the Lincoln Way yard was located at Lincoln Way at 13th Avenue. At times 7 and 17 lines were serviced there, but the yard had little facilities.

(Left) A peak hour scene at Third, Geary and Market. Note Geary car trying to squeeze into the parade heading for the Ferry Loop, in 1939. *Tom Gray collection.* (Below) East of Ninth at Hayes looking down Market with its four street car tracks. Hotel Whitcomb on right, March 28, 1938. *Ted Wurm collection.*

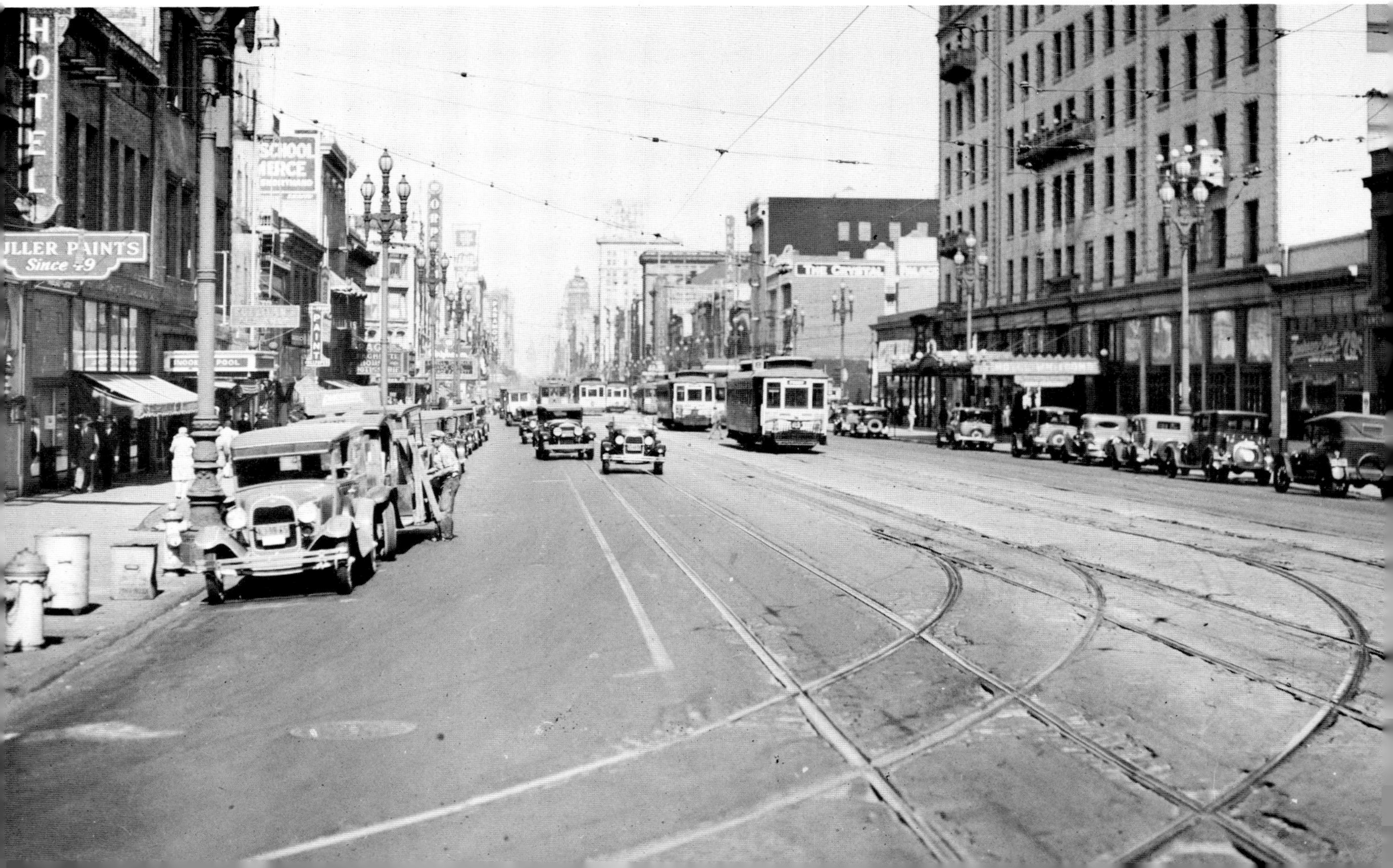

McAllister Street car house was bounded by Central, Fulton, Masonic and McAllister. Lines #5 and #21 were assigned to this barn. Note #5 line cuts diagonally on a private right-of-way from Fulton to McAllister Street. ***Tom Gray photo.***

In 1933, in the midst of a nationwide depression the railway sought to repeal the two-man car ordinance to cut losses. While one-man operation had not been in effect on any line since the tragic wreck in 1918, one-man operation was again instituted on the Visitacion Valley line in San Mateo County. The county had no restrictions on one-man car operation. Assigned to the Visitacion line was rebuilt car #285, which came out of Elkton shops on May 11, 1932. In anticipation that one-man cars would be okayed, brand new #989 was built as a one-man, two man car. A temporary injunction was obtained in 1934. The railway then converted many cars for one-man, two man operation with the first car rolling on Folsom Street line, March 13, 1935. Elkton shops became a busy place. A total of 135 cars were so converted. Meanwhile, several cars already of the one-man car type were purchased from eastern U.S.A. cities where these cars had become surplus. One-man cars were adopted on lines south of Market Street and crosstown lines, 19, 22 along with Third Street lines. Market and Mission Streets, because of the heavy travel remained as two-man cars.

The City of San Francisco, however, continued their legal battle and in 1938 won out. The court gave the Market Street Railway six months to comply, so by February, 1939, all lines were was back to two-man. Two-man operation did not apply to motor coaches, so the weaker travelled street car lines started to disappear rapidly in favor of buses. It was not until 1954, that voters okayed the one-man car operation, but by that time only five street car lines remained in San Francisco.

The following street cars were converted and operated in one-man car service: 180, 265, 266-305, 778, 800-825, 837-838, 850-884, 941-962, 989, and 991-994. Cars 180, 265 and 285 were rebuilt as one-man only. The above along with 402-410, 725-736 and 740-759 purchased from eastern cities gave a total of 174 cars. Single truck one-man cars 601-605, 613-616 and earlier cars 1023 and 1024 had already been scrapped.

While one-man operation became a dead issue in San Francisco, it was used on the San Mateo line from Daly City (County line) to San Mateo during and after the war in off-peak hour periods. Through cars into San Francisco remained two-man for the entire distance.

In 1938 came another paint scheme. Pre-1938, the car body was green with yellow striping and lettering, the ends were white with black numbers along with a light gray roof and yellow route numbers. Post 1938, saw a drastic change. The front became completely white, the side letterboard white, a wide white streamline flourish adorned the sides with yellow trim along with modernize numbering and a bright yellow

(Above) Obtaining a temporary injunction in 1935 to allow the use of one-man cars, the Market Street Railway rebuilt a number of cars to one-man, two-man operation. Three were changed to one-man only: #265, #285 and #180 as shown above. In 1939 the court ruled in favor of two-man operation, so #180 went into storage. Rebuilt to two-man when Muni took over in 1944. ***Will Whittaker photo.*** **(Center) In 1938 another paint design came to the Market Street Railway. The front became completely white and wide white streamline flourish with yellow trim adorned the sides. The roof was a bright yellow and the numbers had a modern look. Only a limited number in the 201-305, 778-994 series received this treatment.** ***Will Whittaker photo.*** **(Bottom) Car #943 at Ocean Beach during World War II. Note appeal on side of car for trolley "pilots".** ***Guido collection.***

Always a busy place was the 3rd and Townsend Southern Pacific Station. The structure was built in 1915 to commemorate the Panama-Pacific Exposition. The old station built in 1889 was moved south one block as can be seen in the background. The rush of commuters came in 1955 when 16,500 would pour through the station twice each day. Nine street car lines served this station at the peak period. *Smallwood collection.*

roof. Many had a visor placed above the center front window. A good many of the cars never made it to the new color scheme account World War II.

"Long live the five cent fare" went the way of nickel cigar and the five cent ferry in the year 1938. The Railroad Commission authorized a seven cent fare or four tokens for a quarter on May 9, to assist the financial plight of the ailing transit system. The full seven cent fare went into effect on January 1, 1939 or five tokens for 35 cents. The Municipal Railway remained at five cents, which, of course, resulted in fierce competion for the private railway. On November 20, 1943, the Railroad Commission, citing poor service, ordered the fare reduced to six cents, which was to go into effect on December 20, 1943. This directive ended up in the courts. In the meantime the Commission directed the railway to issue one-cent refund coupons for each seven cents fare collected, a nuisance that placed a further burden on the railway. It all ended when the voters of the City and County of San Francisco elected to purchase the entire Market Street Railway, which sale took effect, September 29, 1944. Thereafter the fare also went to seven cents on the San Francisco Municipal Railway.

One of the big route changes came on January 15, 1939, with the opening of the street car terminus at the East Bay Terminal. This terminal was built for the electric trains of the East Bay as their San Francisco destination as they came off the newly constructed Bay Bridge. Half of the street cars would turn off Market at First and proceed the one block to the new terminal, while the other half would continue to the Ferry Loop. The first day was a colossal snafu with cars lined up for blocks. It took several days to straighten out the mess by educating street car operators and the public as to which cars went where.

World War II was a grueling test for the Market Street Railway. Many employees went off to war, so the company had to go all-out in advertising for platform and repair personnel. Many women became motormen, conductors or maintenance employees. As the war continued the Market Street Railway became hard pressed to keep going. The equipment was beat, some just collapsed in the streets. In desperation the voters in 1944 gave the okay to purchase the railway for $7.5 million; $2 million in cash and the rest from future earnings. The "yes" vote won handily, so at 5:00 a.m., September 29, 1944, 440 street cars of the Market Street Railway came under Muncipal Railway ownership, along with 217.034 miles of track of which 28.06 was in San Mateo County. Of the 440 street cars, 338 were operable, 28 in for repairs, 74 beyond repair and could only be classed as junk. (Also included in the sale were a number of other transit vehicles: cable cars, trolley buses, motor coaches and other appurtenances thereto.

Of all the double-truck street cars that operated on the streets of San Francisco by the United Railroads and the Market Street Railway that followed, only #974 was saved for museum purposes. However, it was destroyed by fire while being restored. The body of car #798 was discovered in the gold-rush town of Columbia, California. It is now receiving extensive rebuilding, which, when accomplished, will again provide a bit of the glorious "white front" era. *Will Whittaker photo.*

The following Market Street Railway street cars went to the San Francisco Municipal Railway:

Numbers:	
101-180, except 123 (#123 had been scrapped)	79
201-265	65
266-305	40
736, 737	2
740-749	10
778-994	217
1225, 1227-1238, 1241-1244	17
1553, 1572, 1583, 1595, 1599, 1715, 1716, 1722, 1731	9
San Francisco (Private car)	1
Total	440

As soon as the war was over, V-J Day, August 14,1945, the slashing of the old Market Street Railway street cars got under way with conversion to motor coaches. In just a few short years, the end came on July 3, 1949, with the discontinuance of the last remaining lines; 1,2,3,8 and 31. The scrap yard at Elkton shops became a busy place. The last car to go was #974. This car was donated to the Bay Area Electric Association on January 20, 1950. It operated on a farewell trip, March 19, 1950. It was intended for a planned museum at Rio Vista, California. However, fire, while in a storage area east of Stockton, California, destroyed the car before it could become a museum piece. It is sad to note that one of the hundreds of double truck street cars that existed on the Market Street Railway throughout the many years, not one exist today. A shell of #798 was located in the Sierra foothills and it is now being rebuilt at Duel Vocational Institute at Tracy, California. When completely restored, car #798 will be a remembrance of the days when the White Front cars were a way of life on the streets of San Francisco, where they served the City well for over 50 years.

SAFETY MARKET STREET RY. CO. COURTESY SERVICE

SUNDAY PASS

GOOD ONLY IN SAN FRANCISCO

Good from 6 A. M. on Date of Issue to 5 A. M. the Following Morning

FEBRUARY 2 1941

PRICE — 25 CENTS

This Pass entitles bearer to ride on all cars of this Company except San Mateo Suburban Cars. Where minimum fare in San Francisco is 10 cts. it will be necessary to deposit 5 cts. in addition to Pass, within the city limits of San Francisco. It must remain in the possession of the same passenger during the entire trip and be exhibited to the conductor any time on demand. Not to be lifted by conductor unless conditions are violated.

20 6912 Market St. Railway Co.

NOT REDEEMABLE (SEE OTHER SIDE)

PASS MUST BE PUNCHED BY CONDUCTOR FOR EACH RIDE

CHAPTER 2

MARKET STREET RAILWAY CO. - (UNITED RAILROADS)

THE ELECTRIC STREET CARS

Since electric traction came to San Francisco in the year 1892 the roster of street cars climbed by leaps and bounds. By the turn of the century there were at least 400 cars with the greater majority the single truck variety. Under the Market Street Railway at the time there were approximately twenty routes. Each route had its own color scheme for the cars, so for patrons it was easy to indentify which car to board. When United Railroads took over in 1902, the 414 street cars were painted red and cream with the previous car colors then used on the designation dash on the front of the car. After 1906, the cars were painted Pullman green. To dig into the records of the cars in this era was impossible as much of the records were lost in the earthquake and fire, April 18, 1906. Our rosters of cars begins with the reign of United Railroads. Not included are many single truck and double truck cars of the early days which were scrapped up to and including the 1910 period. All in all this listing will show just under one thousand cars that came under United Railroads and Market Street Railway ownership from 1902 to the San Francisco Muncipal Railway take over in the year 1944.

1-12 On a tour of street car builder facilities to order new cars or search for any available after the disastrous earthquake and resulting fire, April 18, 1906, President Patrick Calhoun of United Railroads spotted these large suburban cars sitting on the St. Louis Car Company property. Ordered by the Philadelphia & Western Railway and built the year before, the company had gone broke. Calhoun saw these heavy suburban cars as just the ticket for the San Mateo line, which would soon see severe competition from Southern Pacific upon completion of their Bayshore cut-off set for 1908. He bought 12 "Big Subs," as they became known, on the spot plus four trailers. The latter were sold to Northern Electric, upon their arrival in San Francisco (the trailers were motorized and became part of the Sacramento Northern in later years). After adjustments to flanges and motor casings the "Big Subs" settled in on the San Mateo line. Reluctantly they were taken out of service in 1923 and offered for sale. After ten long years in storage, six were scrapped at Elkton shops. Two years later the remaining six met the same fate with #10 the last to go, August 9, 1935.

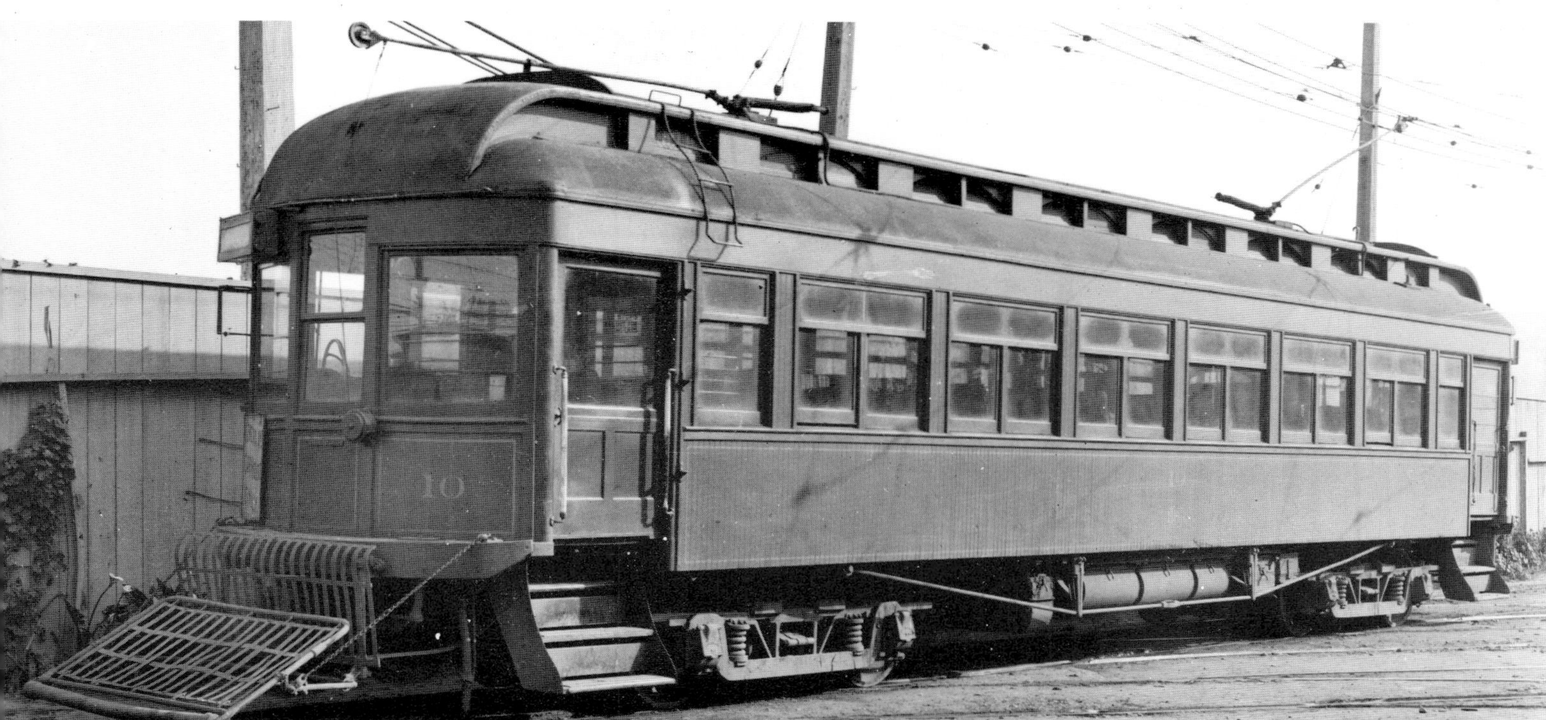

Car #10 ready for its run on the San Mateo line. These impressive cars with comfortable leather seats were a true interurban transit vehicle. They were dubbed "Big Subs" and performed the best of service until their appetite for electrical power did them in during the latter part of 1923. ***United Railroads.***

45

This car was an odd ball. Built in 1900 for the San Francisco & San Mateo Railway, it was one of ten, numbered 41-50. When United took over in 1902, these cars were given numbers 671-680. They were renumbered again in 1904 and again in 1908 when the number 45 was reassigned this car. Generally it was used as a relief car for the Olivet cemetery car when it needed shopping. It was the last in its original state as a double truck car to run in San Francisco. Scrapped January 19, 1926. For additional details see 671-680 group on roster page.

Photo taken at the Geneva barn. Of the ten cars of this type taken over from the San Francisco & San Mateo Railway in 1902, it was the only one to remain in its original state until scrapped in January, 1926. In later years used as a relief car when the Olivet cemetery car needed repair. ***Tom Gray collection.***

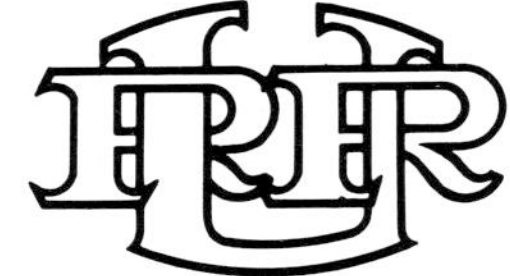

101-180

Built by the Jewett Car Company in 1911. They were the first cars purchased with the Pay As You Enter system. They received a zero rating from the riding public; longitudinal rattan seats throughout with no smoking compartment. They were assigned to the Sutter 1-2-3 lines and in 1914 shifted to the 6-7-17 Haight street lines. In 1916 about a half dozen cars were rebuilt with a four window open section on one end, but were closed again when the seat modernization program took place in 1927 for all this type car. The "Jewett's" immediately jumped to a big plus for their riding qualities offering deep cushion cross seats throughout and a smoking compartment. In 1935, car No. 180 was altered to a one-man car for south of Market lines, but when the one-man car was outlawed in 1939, the unit went into storage until the Muni takeover in 1944, when it was restored to its former two-man car status. Under the Muni, after 1944, the cars started to appear on many of the south of Market lines and of all places on the Muni "H" line. Account conflicting numbers with Muni cars, many of the 100's were renumbered into the 400 series. All were gone by the end of 1949.

(Above) Car #109 one of 80 cars purchased from the Jewett Car Company in 1922. These cars initiated the Pay As You Enter system in 1911. ***United Railroads.***

(Below) During the one-man car era 1935-1939, Car #180 was the only one of this class to be rebuilt into strictly a one-man car. After Muni took over in 1944, the car was changed back to its original appearance as a two-man car. ***Will Whittaker photo.***

201-265

Built by the American Car Company, St. Louis, in 1913, these cars were the best in design to meet San Francisco's needs. Known as the California type with an open section on each end and a closed center section, they became the prototype for ordering new street cars for several decades, including the San Francisco Municipal Railway. The open sections had wooden cross seats and the center section rattan longitudinal seating. After the 1927 uplift program the cars were all enclosed with outer sections having rattan cross seating and center section deep cushion cross seats. As received in 1913, they were assigned to the Sutter 1-2-3 lines, which for the most part is where they stayed during their existence. In 1935, car No. 265 became a one-man car. When the one-man operation was declared illegal in 1939, the car went into storage. Under the Muni takeover in 1944, the car was restored to its former appearance. The cars were popular and well maintained with the result that most cars went all the way to 1950 before they were scrapped. Many saw service on Muni's Geary "C" line in 600 series numbers after the Muni takeover.

(Above) Known as the California type it became the prototype for all new street cars in San Francisco for the next several decades. Car #206, built by the American Car Company in 1911, poses for a company photo out on the #12 line. ***United Railroads.***

(Below) Car #265 as a one man car. Note rear door exit. One other car #180 had this one-man car arrangement. Converted back to two-man when Muni took over in 1944. ***Art Lloyd Photo.***

266-305

Starting in 1920 and following the design of the 201 class "California Comfort Cars," and ambitious program of building new street cars was started at Elkton Shops. The first car, #266, was delivered on June 10, 1920. These cars were lighter in construction than the 201 class design. The bodies were new, but trucks, brake equipment and much of the electrical material were salvaged from the 1301 class cars then being scrapped. New cars rolled out at the rate of two per month. With the State of California celebrating its golden jubilee in 1925, it was decided to shift to blue and gold (bright yellow) colors in honor of the event. Public support was unanimous, so cars that were to be numbered #299 -#305, came out in the new colors as #2001 - #2007. However, the new livery was short-lived, as the Market Street Railway went for the white front design. By October, 1927, the blue and gold colors were gone and #2001 - #2007 were changed to their original planned numbers #299-#305. For the South San Francisco line, car #285 was rebuilt to a one-man car with its rear entrance doors removed and paneled over. Also, cars #266 - #284, #286 - #305 were converted to one-man, two-man operations by placing air-operated doors at both loading ends. When the South San Francisco line ended, December 31, 1938, car #285 was rebuilt back to original two-man car status. When Muni took over in 1944, the numbering conflicted with their own, so eleven received 600 numbers. The first scrapped was #290, May 19, 1945, and the last written off, January 31, 1949.

(Above) In 1920 United Railroads started building its own street cars with the California type design. Elkton shops produced over 250 well constructed street cars before the program was concluded in 1933. Car #279 shown here at the Ferry Terminal, February 28, 1939. ***Bert Ward photo.***

(Below) To commemorate California's Golden Jubilee in 1925, Market Street Railway produced the blue and gold (yellow) 2000 series. Car #2001 at the Geneva car barn. There were a total of 14 cars in this livery. It was short-lived, as in less than two years the color scheme reverted back to green sides along with white fronts. The 14 cars assumed their original intended numbers #299-305; 837-843. ***Tom Gray collection.***

(Above) Just out of the Elkton shops, May 11, 1932, as converted to a one-man car for the South San Francisco line in San Mateo county which allowed one-man car operation. Note rear door has side extended in its place. The line ended December 31, 1938. ***Tom Gray photo.***

(Below) In 1939 car #285 was rebuilt back to a two-man car. Shown at the East Bay Terminal in new white flourish design. ***Bert Ward photo.***

401

With the idea of a low floor design powered by four small motors, United constructed an experimental car at their Elkton Shops in 1914. The 47-foot car with 50 seats was built along the lines of the 201 class California Comfort car. Numbered #301, it was one of the best built. It was given a good deal of hoop-la when it went into service on the #8 Market Street line on January 4, 1915. But it soon became apparent that it could hardly pull its own weight let alone a load of passengers. It was relegated to advertising baseball games with large billboards on its sides. On March 10, 1925 it took on the number #401. Two years later it was on the Howard Street line where it struggled along for eight years. With the start of the one-man car episode, #401 went into storage and just about forgotten. In July, 1941 it made its last trip under its own power to Elkton shops where it was scrapped, July 30, 1941. What a museum piece this car would have made!

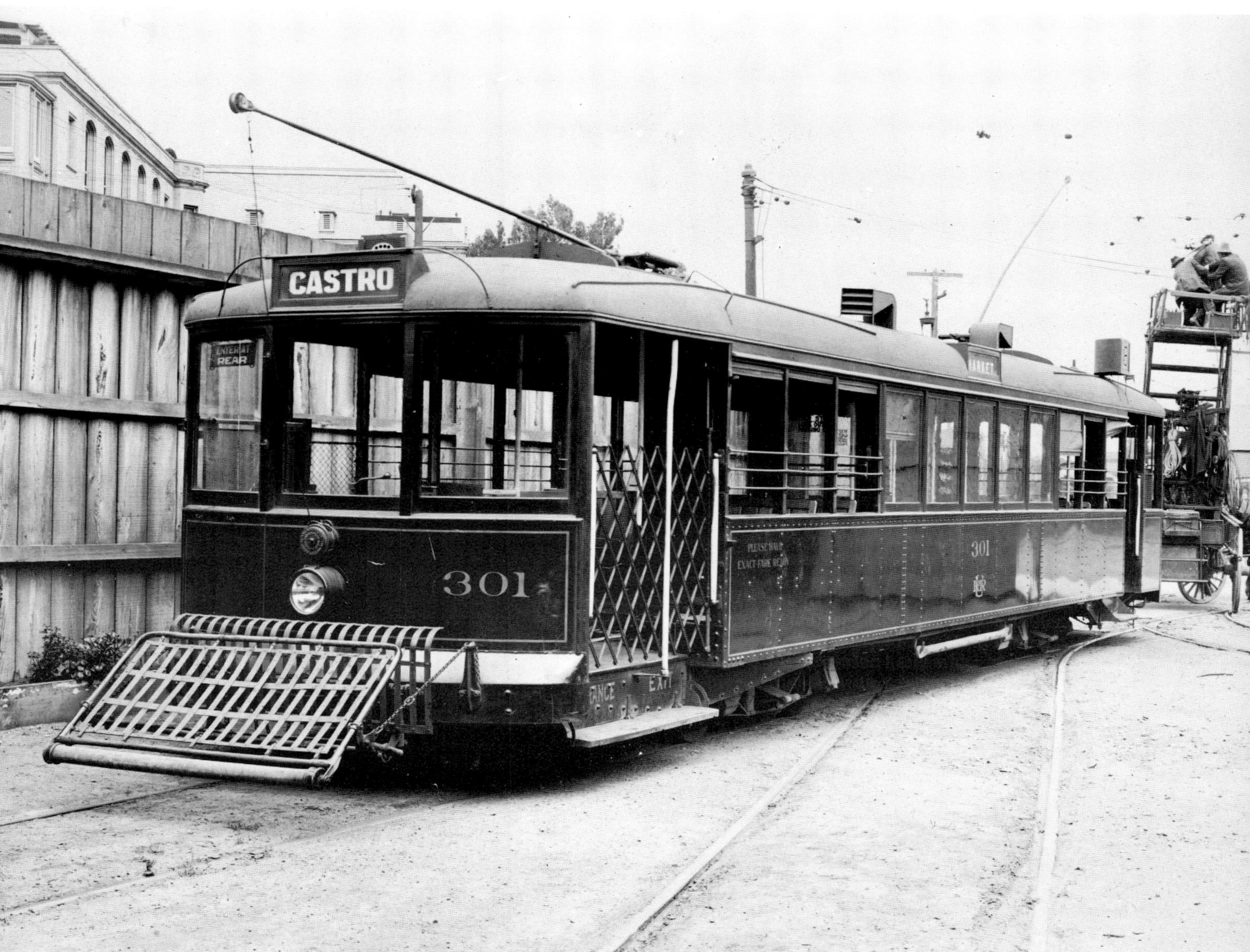

Car #301 as built, July 12, 1915. It had an excellent design with its drop platform, but was badly underpowered. ***United Railroads.***

(Above) Car #301 with a good morning load for downtown as it heads down outer Market Street in the year 1916. *Guido collection.*

(Below) Renumbered #401 on March 10, 1925, the car struggled along on the Howard Street line for eight years before being placed in storage. Photo shows car on its last trip -at 29th and Mission heading for Elkton shops and the scrap dock. July, 1941. *Bert Ward photo.*

402-406

With the advent of one-man cars in 1935, management started looking in eastern cities where such cars were available for sale. This group of five were found on the East St. Louis & Suburban Railway. Built 1927 by the St. Louis Car Company, they were known as "Rail Sedans" for their streamline appearance and comfortable ride. Arriving in 1936 they were assigned to the Howard Street line. Their life in San Francisco was short-lived. When the one-man cars were outlawed in 1939, they went into storage. All were scrapped in the Fall of 1941.

A "Rail Sedan" with its streamline appearance. Car #402 at the Mission Ferry Terminal, July 18, 1938, as a one-man car. ***Bert Ward photo.***

407-410

Also included in the purchase from the East St. Louis & Suburban Railway were these four cars built by the St. Louis Car Company in 1924. In contrast to the Rail Sedans, these cars were of heavier construction, which produced a hard ride and were more noisy as they ambled along the Howard Street line. Their life in San Francisco was also short-lived. When one-man operation became illegal in 1939, the cars went into storage and scrapped in October, 1941.

Purchased in 1936, car #407 and its three sisters had a short life of service in San Francisco, only three years when one-man cars were outlawed. At Ferry terminal, February 2, 1939, the last day of the car's operation is at hand. ***Bert Ward photo.***

601-662

This series was assigned to the best of remaining single truck cars that were in existence in 1912 with all others disposed of. With the beginning of the Market Street Railway in 1893 and the takeover by United Railroads in 1902, it was found impossible to follow the history of all the single truck cars of several hundred that existed in that period. They were not numbered consecutively, but in groups from 551 to 1224. With records destroyed in the earthquake and fire, April 18, 1906, there was no way to obtain accurate disposition lists. Many of these cars were sold for houses, sheds, to other transit companies and a number converted into work cars. The most interesting operation for these cars was the steep two-block section on Fillmore between Broadway and Green Streets. Built in 1895, this section required an underground counter-balance system. Only the single truck cars with a hook on device could be used. When United Railroads took over in 1902, they split the line with the single truck cars operating from Broadway north to Bay and later Marina and double truck south of Broadway. To handle the crowds going to the 1915 Exposition, fourteen cars were rebuilt so they could operate as multiple units (623-626, 632, 641-642, 648-649, 651-654, 658). In 1921 cars 621-627 were again rebuilt with closed ends and four folding doors. #626 kept its wire gates but was rarely used. The author recalls the strange feeling of having the controller open on the descent, but necessary to pull the opposing car uphill. The line was discontinued, April 5, 1941. This ended the single truck car era in San Francisco for the Market Street Railway that had lasted one year short of 50 years.

Single truck car #625, one of the 62 that United Railroads saved for the small lines in 1912. ***Bert Ward photo.***

Single truck car #625 was rebuilt in 1921 for counter-balance service on the Fillmore hill line. ***Guido collection.***

(Above) Single truck car #626. Note gripping device on front end. After rebuilding of several cars on this line, #626 was kept as a spare and only used on rare occasions, but did get the white front treatment in 1925. *Muni photo.* (Below) because of the two-block steep hill on Fillmore between Green and Broadway, a counterbalance system was required to assist electric street cars up and down this hill. The unit shown; numbered 02 was filled with bricks for weight and a hooking device. It brought up the last car at night and the first down in the morning on the counterbalance mechanism. This contraption was parked at the bottom of the hill on Fillmore and Green at night, with a red lantern affixed. In the daytime, it was stored at the Fillmore car barn. *Guido collection.*

671-680

Built by the Hammond Car Company in 1900 for the San Francisco & San Mateo Railway and numbered 41-50. These cars were taken over by United Railroads when it was formed in 1902 and given numbers 671-680. In 1904, three went to South San Francisco Railway & Power Company, numbered 1-3; in 1905, two to U.S. Mail Service "D" and "E"; in 1906, one car to Reno Traction and one to Olivet Cemetery Ass'n. In 1908 five remaining cars were renumbered 44-48. #44, 46-48 rebuilt to PAYE cars in 1919 and given numbers 727-730. See this series for disposition. **See #45 on preceding page for its disposition.**

(Previous page above) Taken over from the San Francisco & San Mateo Railway one of the ten cars placed in the 671 series. Car #672 was converted to Mail car "E" in 1905. Earthquake and resulting fire destroyed the car, April 18, 1906. ***Gil Kneiss collection. (Previous page below)*** **Car #687 became #46 in 1908 and leased to South San Francisco Railway & Power Company. Photo shows car on South San Francisco line in 1917.** ***Tom Gray collection.*** **(Above) Mail car "D" at the Ferry Building ex #671 in the early part of 1906. A few weeks later the earthquake struck, April 18, 1906. The resulting fire caught this car on Mission Street near the post office and it was totally destroyed.** ***Tom Gray collection.***

UNIT... OF SAN FRANCISCO

JAN.	FEB.	MAR.	APR.	MAY	JUNE	JULY	AUG.	SEPT.	OCT.	NOV.	DEC.

1	2	3	4	5	6	7	8	9	10	11	12	13	14	15	16
17	18	19	20	21	22	23	24	25	26	27	28	29	30	31	

MAIL DOCK LINE TRANSFER
Not Transferable
Good only this day, and for continuous ride on first car passing transfer point after time punched.
G. F. CHAPMAN,
General Manager

WESTBOUND TO	2nd N	Bryant W at Second	3rd N or S

HOUR	A.M.	1	2	3	4	5	6	7	8	9	10	11	12	WEST BOUND
MINUTE		10		20		30		40		50		S	X	
HOUR	P.M.	1	2	3	4	5	6	7	8	9	10	11	12	

681-698

Built in 1900 for the San Francisco & San Mateo Railway by the St. Louis Car Company and numbered 51-70. United took over these cars in 1902. #61 rebuilt into private car "San Francisco," and #67 into Funeral Car #2. The rest renumbered 681-698. #696 was extensively damaged by a "Big Sub" runaway in 1908 and rebuilt to wrecker #0507. #698 became 2nd #696 in 1915. All extensively rebuilt in 1915 to three-compartment PAYE type cars. All scrapped in 1926-1927.

Car #683 at the Kentucky Street (later 3rd Street) car barn about the year 1912. *Bert Ward collection.*

The 681-698 series were extensively rebuilt in 1915 at Elkton shops to three-compartment PAYE cars as can be attested by this photo of car #691. *Richard Schlaich collection.*

A rare photo of this car #698 at 3rd and Market, 1914. A year later this car was rebuilt with others of this series and became 2nd #696, as 1st #696 had been demolished by a "Big Sub" in 1908. ***Bert Ward collection.***

2nd 698-699 In the good old days, viewing the City by sightseeing street cars. San Francisco had two of them. The first built in 1900 by the Market Street Railway's shop at 28th & Valencia was name "City of Atlanta" and soon changed to "Golden Gate" when United took over in 1902. The second car, built by United in 1904, took on the name "California." With motor buses coming into the picture, the cars were sadly discontinued after the Fair in 1915. They were rebuilt into street cars numbered 698 and #699. Scrapped in 1925.

hortly after the 1915 Exposition this sightseeing car named "Golden Gate" was rebuilt into a reet car #698 (no photo found). Ten years later its usefullness ended. Scrapped in 1925. hoto taken in the year 1904. ***From Muni files.***

701-724

Constructed by United Railroads in 1911-1912. Bodies were new, but much of the early 900, 1000, 1100, 1200's supplied the underframes, motors and controls as they were being scrapped at the time. First car out was numbered 700, but changed to #712 to keep with the practice of the last digit starting with one. These sturdy cars with high quality interiors originally had open ends with center section enclosed, but all were completely enclosed in the 1920's. The cars had wooden seats in the end sections and longitudinal rattan seats in the center. All were retired in 1935.

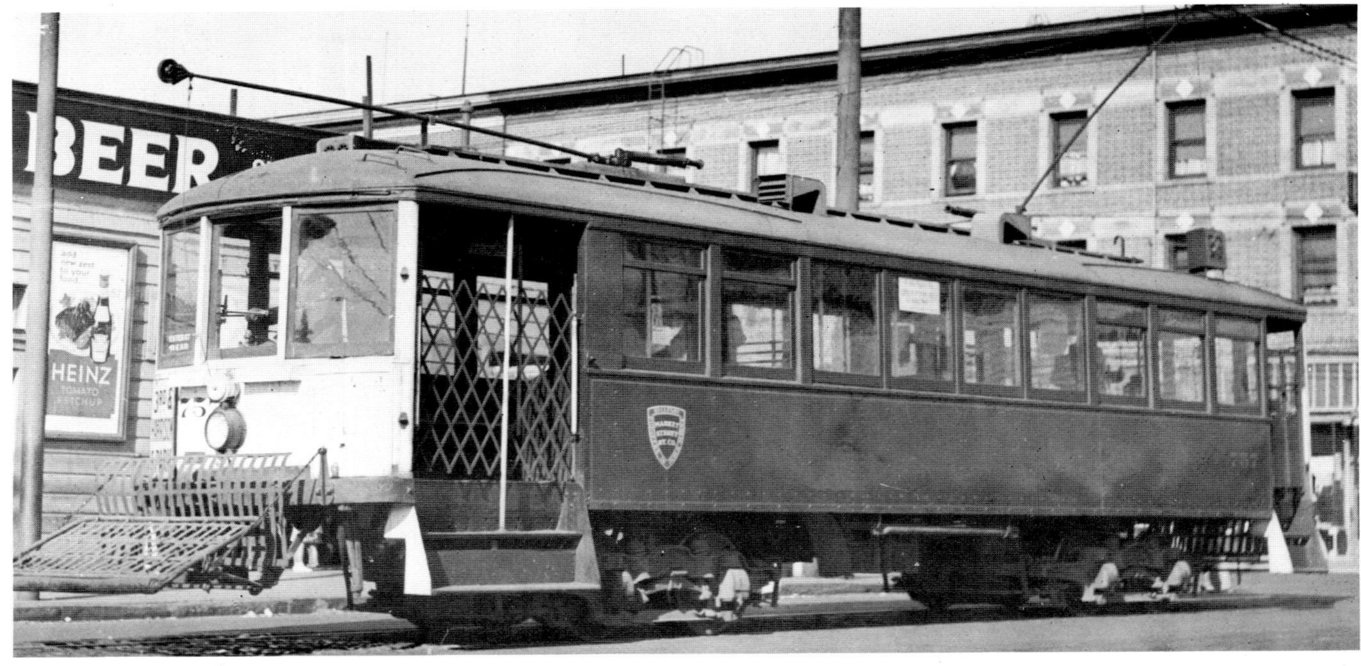

Car #710 fresh out of the paint shop in 1925 with its new white front design, green sides and Byllesby logo. Note end sections have been closed in.

1st 725-726

Built by Hammond Car Company in 1895. They were part of an order of 25 for the Mission Street line. Numbers 1022-1024 were rebuilt into one-man PAYE cars in 1914 to be used on the Visitacion line. After a bad accident on that line in 1918, which demolished #1022, the #1023 and #1024 were again rebuilt into two-man cars and numbered 725-726. Retired in 1922. Once again they were in the Elkton shop. With new bodies, but using the old motors, controls, etc., they emerged as California Comfort cars. In the Fall of 1923 they were renumbered 784 and 785. They remained in service until after the Muni take over in 1944 -scrapped in July, 1946.

(Previous page lower) 1023 as she looked in 1914 after being rebuilt into a one-man car for the Visitacion Valley line. In 1918 rebuilt again and came out as car #725. Again in 1923 discarding the body, the car emerged as #784, retaining the old motors, trucks and controls. (Above and below) The same treatment was accorded a sister unit #1024, which went to #726 thence #785. Both cars came under Muni in 1944 and lasted until July 5, 1946 when they were scrapped. *Tom Gray collection.*

1st 727-730

Originally San Francisco & San Mateo Railway. Built by Hammond Car Company in 1900. See 671-680 series. Became United #44, 46-48. Rebuilt in 1919 to PAYE cars. Of note, they were the smallest double truck cars to see service in San Francisco. Used very little. Scrapped in 1927.

Originally in the 671 series, leased to South San Francisco Railway & Power Company as their #48. Returned and rebuilt as PAYE car along with three others and numbered 727-730. Photo taken at Chestnut and Sansome in 1919. Scrapped in 1927. ***Tom Gray collection.***

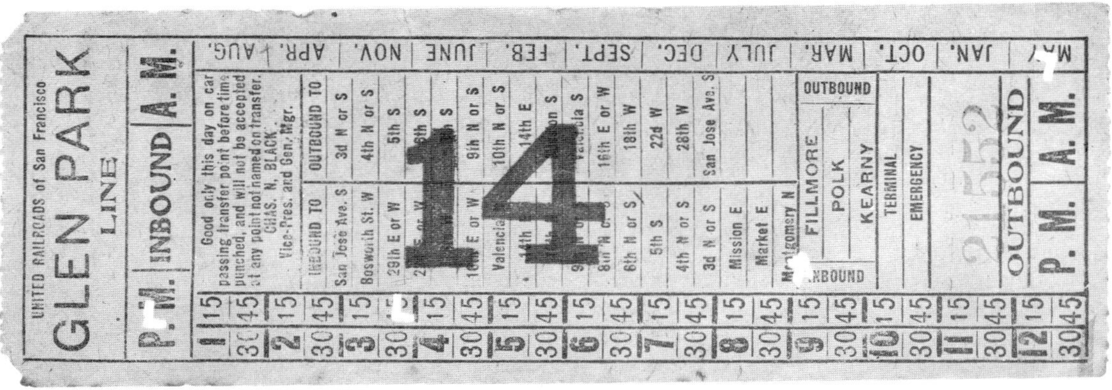

1st 731-745

After the takeover by United Railroads of the Sutter Street Railway in 1902, which two years before had taken over the Sutter Railroad, 15 cars of the original California type came under United's ownership. The cars built by W.L. Holman Car Co., of San Francisco took on the numbers 731-745. They were rebuilt in 1915-16 to California type PAYE cars with a two-window open section on one end, three on the other and a five-window enclosed center section. All were retired around 1925.

(Above) Originally belonged to Sutro Railway Company and came into United Railroads in 1902. Car #740 still in its original construction on the #25 San Bruno line, August 17, 1915.

(Below) Soon after taken to Elkton shops and built into a PAYE type car such as #742. ***United Railroads.***

1st 746

A loner. Built by St. Louis Car Company in 1896, as a private parlor car and given the name HERMOSA. Rebuilt in 1918, as a PAYE car and given the number 746. Scrapped in 1927. No photo of this car has been found.

1st 751-756

Built before the turn-of-the-century for the old Market Street Railway in 1895 by the Hammond Car Company. Originally numbered in the 1000 series. Six of these cars were rebuilt in 1916 to PAYE cars and given the 751-756 numbers. Lasted less than ten years. Gone by 1926.

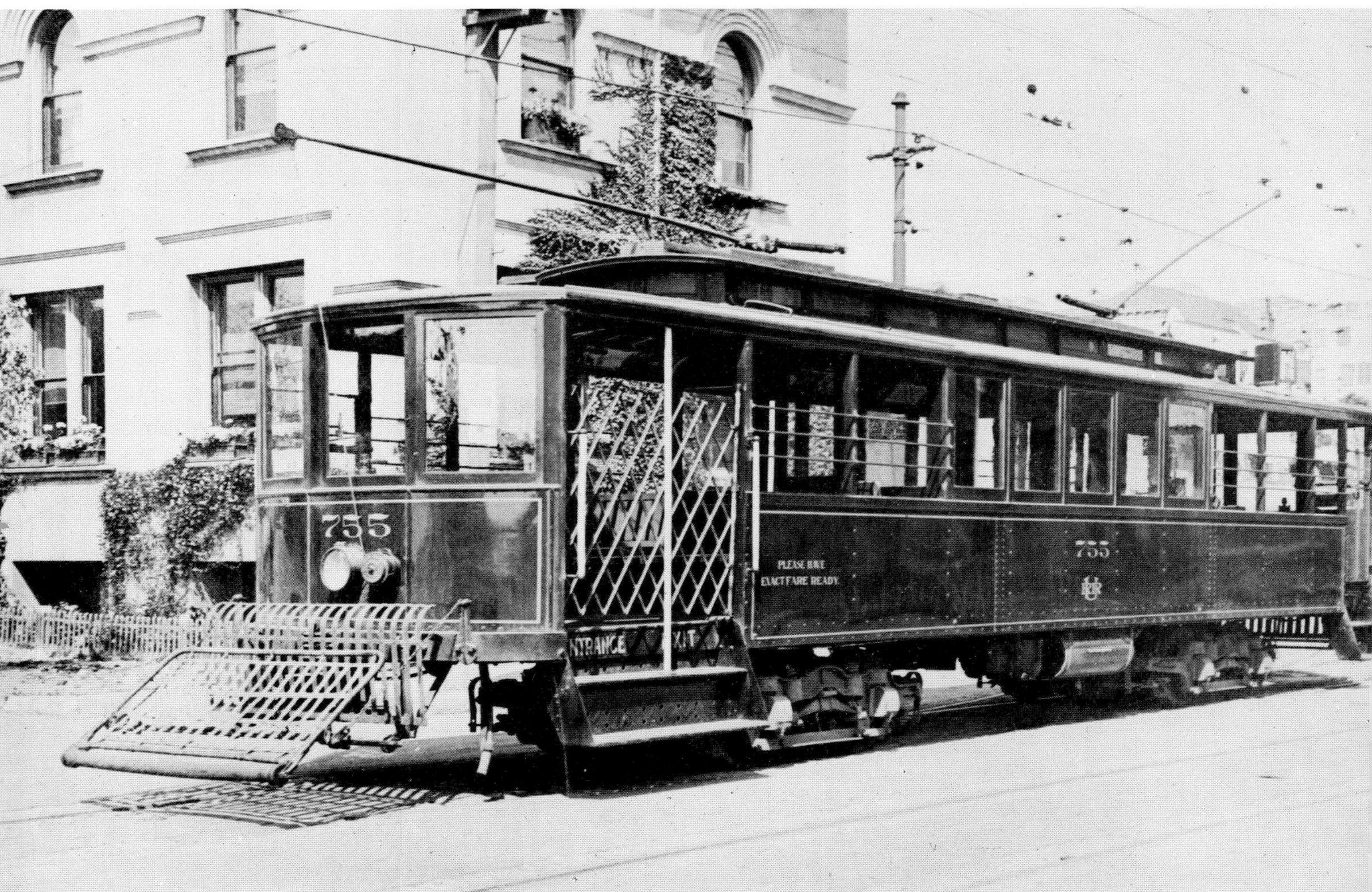

Built in 1895. Car #755 received the PAYE rebuild treatment in 1916 along with four of its sisters. ***Bert Ward collection.***

757-771

Another batch of cars dating back to the 1890's. Built by Hammond Car Co., and placed in the 1000 series for the Mission Street line. In 1918-1919 they were rebuilt to California type PAYE cars and served for a short time on south of Market lines. In 1920 moved to the #33 line for the remainder of their life until this line went trolley bus, October 5, 1935. The cars came out with open end sections but were enclosed in the mid-1920's. The cars had longitudinal seats throughout, which fit into line 33 operation with its switch-back at Market and Clayton Street - no one had to get up and flip seats over or ride backwards. All cars scrapped in 1936, except #765, which was wrecked and scrapped in September, 1927.

(Above) This group of 15 cars were re-built at the Elkton Shops in 1918. After a breaking period on south of Market lines they became permanent on the #33 line. Car #757 at 3rd and Harrison terminous in the early 1930's. ***Bob Stein collection.***

(Below) Car #773 was one of seven out-shopped by United Railroads at their Elkton shops in 1919. Underframes came from old Omnibus Cable Company cars that had been rebuilt for electric service at the turn of the century. With only one partition, wind whipped through the cars, so were nick-named "Pneumonia Specials." Their service was less than ten years. ***Tom Gray collection.***

772-778

With seven underframes obtained from old Omnibus Cable Company electric cars, vintage 1898, Elkton shops in 1919 came out with the 772-778 series of the PAYE type. They were unpopular from the start, as they had only a single partition in the center, which made them very drafty. They soon got the designation of "Pneumonia Specials," by the patrons and platform personnel alike. By mid-1928 they were gone.

2nd 725-734

To augment the one-man car fleet these cars were purchased from the Williamsport Railway, Penna., in June, 1935. They were built by J. G. Brill in 1913 (6) and 1917 (4) numbered 50-59. They were trucked from Baltimore, loaded on ships and headed for Panama Canal and San Francisco. They were in good condition, so it took little to get them in service. When one-man cars ended in 1939, so did these cars. All scrapped July, 1941.

Ex-Williamsport Car #730 trundles along the #30 line at Army and Potrero in one-man car service in the year 1937. *Tom Gray photo.*

2nd 735-736

Also purchased from the Williamsport Railway were two other cars, ex-numbers 42 and 43. Placed on the Visitacion Valley line, July, 1935 and ended when line motorized, July 31, 1937. Placed in storage and for reasons unknown remained in that status for eight years until scrapped under the Muni banner in 1945.

Two purchased Williamsport cars came with arch roofs such as car #736. Photo shows car on the Visitacion Valley line in 1937. *Tom Gray collection.*

2nd 740-754

2nd 755-759

(747-750 1st numbers)

In addition to the nine (402-410) purchased from the East St. Louis & Suburban Railway in April, 1936, these fine twenty cars were also included. They were built by the St. Louis Car Company in 1918. They were identical except the 755-759 were a little over five feet longer, which is obvious with their 12 windows on a side whereas the 740-754 had ten windows. When the one-man car operation was outlawed in 1939, six were modified for two-man use with double doors on each end. The cars were available for any line to assist with crowds expected for the 1939-1940 Golden Gate Exposition that was held on man-made Treasure Island. After the event concluded September 29, 1940, the cars were placed in storage and then scrapped a year later.

(Above) Car #742 at outer end of line, 26th end Mission in the year 1937. ***Ken Kidder photo.***

(Below) Ex St. Louis & Suburban Railway #756 at Ferry Building Mission Terminal in 1937. The group 755-759 were known as the "long" cars, with 12 side windows, while the 740-754 group had ten side windows. ***Bert Ward photo.***

2nd 778 See 2nd #1424 that follows for details.

779-994 This numbering of cars is a continuation of the building of California Comfort cars that began in 1920 with the 265-305 series at Elkton shops. Just why the numbering started at 779, instead of a continuation from 306 is not known. #779 was completed May 21, 1923, with the last in the series, #994, December 28, 1933. #725 and #726, rebuilt in 1922, were given numbers 2nd 784 and 2nd 785 in 1923. Numbers 784 and 785 that had only been in existence a few months were given numbers 792 and 793. Cars #837-843 came out with blue and gold livery numbered 2008 through 2014 in 1925. In less than a year they were returned to their original planned numbers, 837-843 with the advent of the White Front cars. Because of a different gear ratio #923-#941 and #944-#994 were faster operating cars and were assigned to the #31 Balboa line. #989 had the distinction of being built either one-man or two-man car, June 26, 1933. It inaugurated one-man service on the #36 Folsom line, March 13, 1935. Another 70 cars of this group were rebuilt to one-man, two-man cars. When the Muni took over in September, 1944, the entire group was intact. #980 was destroyed by fire, March 29, 1945, and #895 renumbered to take its place. The first to be retired was #902, May 19, 1945. Five years later they were all gone with #974 the last. It was sold to the Bay Area Electric Ass'n for museum purposes. This, however, never came to pass, as the car was destroyed by fire.

(Above) Car #779 assigned to the #11 line is ready to depart from the Ferry Building, Mission terminal, for 24th and Hoffman, March 30, 1939. ***Bert Ward photo.***

(Below) Car #803 ambles inbound on Sloat Blvd. right-of-way just having left the Ocean Beach-Zoo terminal on the #12 line, January 24, 1944. ***Will Whittaker photo.***

Car #953 on the one-man #29 line in 1938 as it heads out 3rd Street near 23rd Street intersection. *Tom Gray photo.*

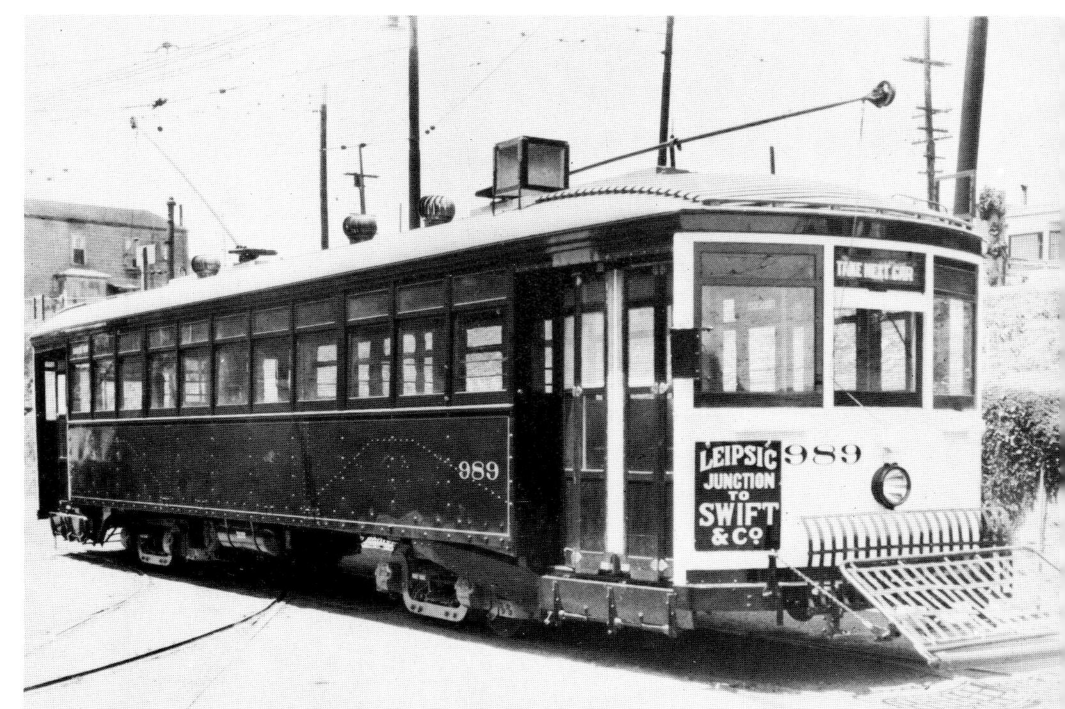

Car #989 was the first street car built as a one-man, two-man car, June 26, 1933. It was assigned to the South San Francisco line. However, when an injunction was obtained against San Francisco's enforcement of the one-man car law, car #989 inaugurated one-man car service on the Folsom Street line, March 13, 1935 Photo taken at Elkton shops. *Tom Gray collection.*

The Elkton paint shop had a different idea as to paint schemes when car #990 appeared for service August 1, 1933. "Special" is the word as it had aluminum ends, roof and poles maroon window sash, green end letterboards and blue car numbers. The sides were the usual green. It did not last long and soon was back to the standard "white front" format. *Tom Gray collection.*

1225-1244

Built by Laclede Car Company, St. Louis, in 1903, these cars were one of the best in riding qualities. Assigned to the 20-mile San Mateo line, the author remembers the many times he rode these fine cars when visiting relatives in San Mateo. Between 1906-1923, the "Big Subs" replaced these cars on the San Mateo line and were assigned to the Mission lines between the Ferry Terminal and Holy Cross Cemetery. When these 20 cars came back to the "40" line in 1923, they had been rebuilt to PAYE type with three compartments, deep cushioned seats with electric heaters. They gave Southern Pacific intense competition. With the Muni take over in 1944, the cars lasted five more years with the final run January 15, 1949. The first, #1225 was scrapped in 1945, the rest followed before the year 1949 was over.

(Above) San Mateo interurban car #1240 at the Ferry Terminal in the mid-1930's. Note car still has ribbed sides. ***Guido collection.***

(Below) Car #1241 at Geneva car barn in the year 1937. Note straight steel sides installed on this car. ***Bert Ward collection.***

1300-1424

This was the first large double-truck order by the United Railroads when they took over in 1902. The cars were delivered in three groups: 1300-1349 (1903), 1350-1374 (1904) and 1375-1424 (1905). They were all built by the St. Louis Car Company. The style was different than cars obtained heretofore. The enclosed center section (1300-1374 had five windows; the 1375-1424, four windows) had longitudinal seats, however, the open end sections had reversible wooden cross seats with screens along the sides. Entrance or exit was via the steps next to the closed sections. They were the finest cars of the times in San Francisco and equipped with air brakes. In 1908 route boxes were installed on the roof. In 1912-13 they were extensively rebuilt at Elkton Shops with solid siding to end sections, changes in roof, fronts and window frames. Windows for the full length were installed in the 1920's. Cars were assigned to any line other than Market Street account protruding steps. Starting 1927 they started to disappear with many of the motors and electrical equipment going into the new cars being built at the time (779-800's). Very few received the white front treatment. The last to go was #1421 in December 1935.

(Above) Car #1389 poses for a full size view company photo at the Geneva car barn, January 22, 1908. ***United Railroads.***

(Below) Ready for service, car #1359 at Geneva car barn, August 16, 1914. ***United Railroads.***

(Above) To get public reaction, United Railroads enclosed car #1313 as shown. Apparently the patrons still liked the open sections as they reamined until the late 1920's. Car #1313 with its new look went into service April 17, 1906. Little did anyone know what was going to happen the next morning at 5:12 a.m. which would lay the city in ruins. ***United Railroads.***

(Below) Car #1367. All of the 1300-1424 group were extensively rebuilt as PAYE cars in 1911-1912 as can be seen from photo. The 1300-1374 cars had a five window closed section, 1375-1424 four. ***United Railroads, Richard Schlaich collection.***

(Above) Side view of rebuilt car #1324 in the late 1910's. 29th & Valencia. *Tom Gray collection.*

(Below) Car #1375 at Geneva car barn, October, 1928. Note white front has been applied. Very few received this treatment. In addition to the car's four center window enclosure, one open section has been enclosed. *Market Street Railway photo.*

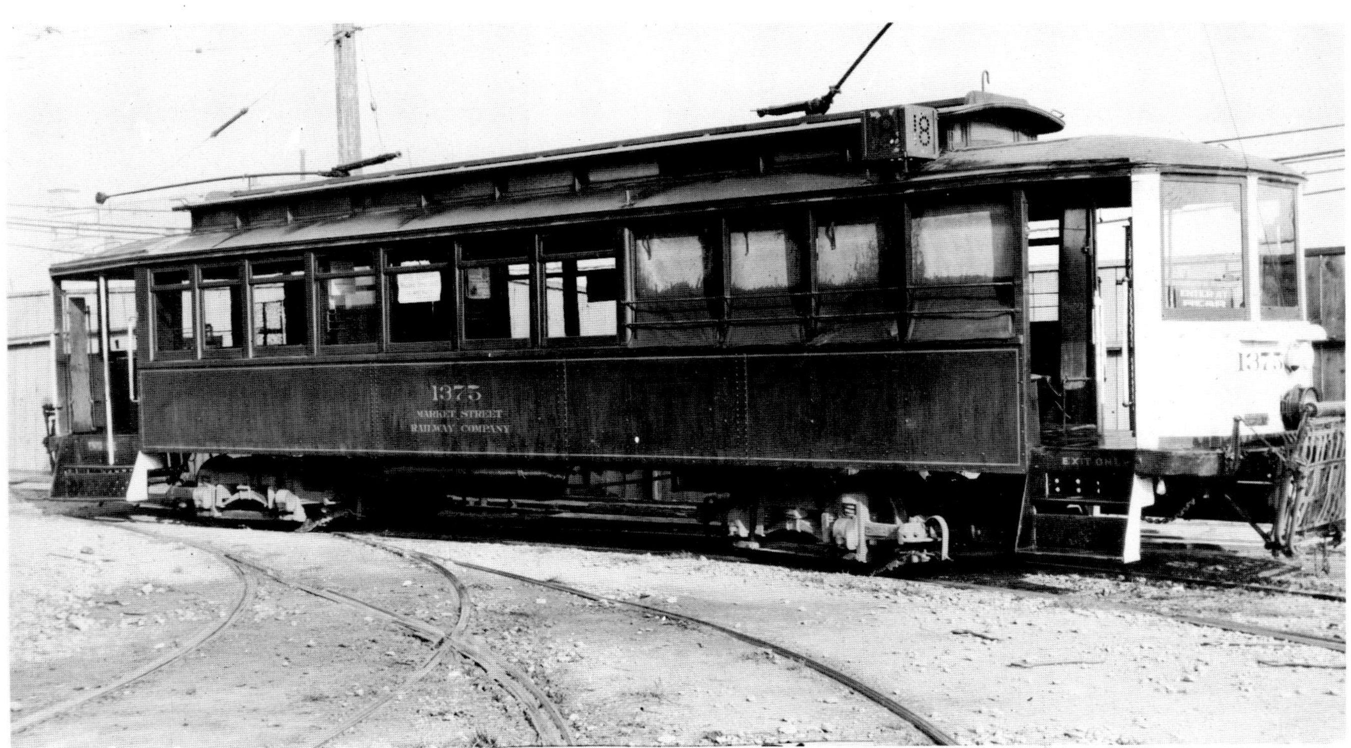

2nd 1350 Built by the Press Steel Car Company on experimental basis. Arrived in 1904, so actually there were two 1350's on the roster at the same time. Removed from service for modifications and idle for several years. Back in service by 1910 taking on the number 1391, which had been vacated as this car had been scrapped account of a wreck. Scrapped in early 1930's.

2nd 1424 Typical of the 201-265 series cars. However, this unit was somewhat different with its entrance and exit doors installed for its service on the South San Francisco line. Outshopped, January 22, 1924 by Elkton Shops, it was given the number 2nd 1424 taking place of the original #1424, which had been renumbered 2nd #1374. When the South San Francisco line went to one-man, May 27, 1934, the car was assigned to the Visitacion Valley line. When that line went one-man a year later, it was back at Elkton Shops. Rebuilt into a one-man car, it emerged as 2nd #778. It came into the Muni ownership in 1944. Scrapped October 3, 1948.

(Above) With shifting of car numbers; #1424 to #1374 the number 1424 became available. Market Street Railway built a 2nd #1424 for the South San Francisco line with interurban type entrance and exit doors as can be seen by this photo taken at Geneva car barn. The car emerged from the Elkton shops, January 22, 1924. ***Tom Gray collection.***

(Right) Front view of car 2nd #1424. Note large headlight required for South San Francisco line. ***Tom Gray collection.***

(Below) Car #778 (ex 2nd #1424) swings into Mission Street from the Embarcadero, May, 1938. ***Will Whittaker photo.***

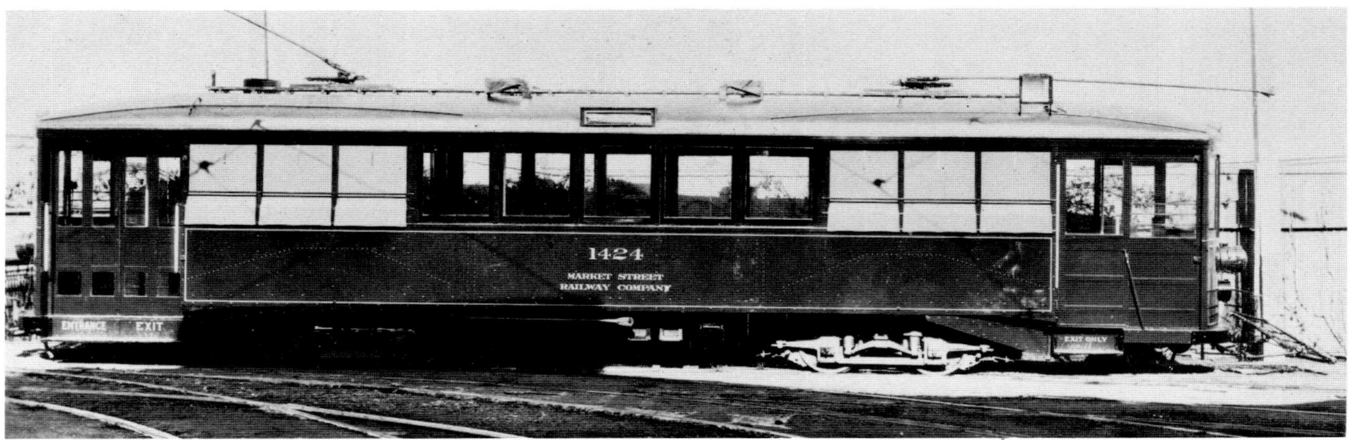

United Railroads of San Francisco.

OBSERVATION CAR "GOLDEN GATE."

Observation Cars in charge of competent guides leave Market, Post and Montgomery Streets, and Market and Second Streets, at 10 A. M. and 2 P. M. daily, Sundays included; returning at 1.30 P. M. and 5.30 P. M.

**See Union Square, City Hall,
Lick Monument, Mechanics Pavilion,
St. Ignatius Church and College,
New Post Office, U. S. Mint, Southern Pacific Hospital,
Mission Dolores, Affiliated Colleges,
Cliff House, Ocean Beach, Etc., Etc.**

Distance, Round Trip, 20 Miles.

THE NEW OBSERVATION CAR "CALIFORNIA."

*Board one of these cars and see San Francisco.
The only trip of its kind.
Passing every principal point of interest.*

**COMPETENT GUIDES IN CHARGE. - - -
PARTICULARLY DESIGNED FOR TOURISTS.**

An instructive, pleasant ride aboard a comfortable and well-equipped car.

SEE FRONT PAGE FOR PARTICULARS.

Distance, Round Trip, 20 miles.

THE PARLOR CAR "HERMOSA."

Handsomely upholstered. Beautifully furnished, seating 30 persons. May be chartered as a party car, at the following rates:

Within City Limits,	*$2.50 per hour.*
During the day,	
Minimum charge,	*$10.00*
Evenings, 7 P. M. to 1 A. M.,	*$12.00*

This Company is prepared to furnish other cars at reasonable rates.

UNITED RAILROADS OF SAN FRANCISCO,

ROOM 822 RIALTO BUILDING,
NEW MONTGOMERY AND MISSION STS.
SAN FRANCISCO, CAL.

G. F. CHAPMAN,
GENERAL MANAGER.

SUBURBAN CAR.

These cars are operated from Fifth and Market sts. direct to San Mateo, passing through Ocean View, Colma, Holy Cross, San Bruno, Tanforan, Millbrae, and Burlingame. Fare (one way), 25 cents. Cars leave as follows:

FROM FIFTH AND MARKET STS., every half hour, commencing at 6 A. M., up to 6.30 P. M., and thereafter at 7.30, 8.30, 9.30, 10.30 and 11.30 P. M.

CARS LEAVE SAN MATEO every half hour after 5.30 A. M. until 7.30 P. M., and thereafter at 8, 9, 10, 11, and 12 P. M. ON SUNDAYS cars leave every 15 minutes between 9 A. M. and 7 P. M.

MARKET STREET RAILWAY ELECTRIC STREET CARS
(United Railroads Roster)

Scr. - Scrapped Reblt - Rebuilt EStL&S - East St. Louis & Suburban Railway.

Numbers	Builder	Date	Remarks - Disposition
1- 12	St. Louis Car Co.	1906	Known as "Big Subs." Used on San Mateo line. Scr. 1933-35.
45		1900	See 671-680 note.
101-180	Jewett Car Co.	1911	#123 wrecked August 30, 1942 and Scr. All other Scr. by 1949. See Note.
201-265	American Car. Co.	1913	Known as "California" type. Scr. between 1947-50. See note
266-285	United Railroads	1920-21	#285 reblt to one-man car (1932) Back to two man (1939) All scr. 1945-49
286-298	Market St. Ry.	1924-25	Scr. 1945-49.
299-305	Market St. Ry.	1925	Built as "Blue Gold" cars #2001-#2007. To #299-305 (1926) Scr. 1946-48.
401	United Railroads	1914	Experimental. Ex #301. To #401 (1925) Storage (1935) Scr. 1941.
402-406	St. Louis Car Co.	1927	Purchased from EStL&S (1936). Known as Rail Sedans. Stored (1939) Scr. (1941).
407-410	St. Louis Car Co.	1924	Purchased from SStL&S (1936). Stored (1939). Scr. (1941).
601-605	Hammond Car Co.	1895	Single Truck. Reblt. one-man car United RR (1914-15). Scr. (1935) See Note.
606-612	Hammond Car Co.	1893	Single Truck. Some Reblt. One-man car. United RR (1914-15) Scr. by 1930. See Note.
617-620	Holman Car Co.	1896	Single Truck. Scr. by 1930. See note.
621-627	Hammond Car Co.	1895	Single Truck. Reblt United RR for Fillmore Hill Service. Scr. (1941) See note.
628-662	Hammond Car Co.	1895	Some reblt. by United RR (1915) All Scr. by 1935. See note.
671-680	Hammond Car Co.	1900	Ex San Francisco & San Mateo Ry #41-50. See note.
681-698	St. Louis Car Co.	1900	Ex San Francisco & San Mateo Ry #51-70. Scr. by 1927. See note.
2nd 698	Market Str. Ry.	1900	Ex Sightseeing car "City of Atlanta". Renamed "Golden Gate". Passenger car #698 (1918) Scr. 1925.
699	United Railroads	1904	Ex Sightseeing car "California". Passenger car (1918) Scr. 1925.
701-724	United Railroads	1911-12	Scr. by 1935
1st 725-726	Hammond Car Co.	1895	From #1023 & #1024 reblt to 2nd #784 and 2nd #785 (1923). Scr. 1946
1st 727-730	Hammond Car Co.	1900	See #671-680 above (Scr. 1927)
1st 731-745	Holman Car Co.	1897	Ex Sutro RR. To Sutter Str. Ry (1900); To United (1902) Scr. mid-1920s.
1st 746	St. Louis Car Co.	1896	Ex Private Car "Hermosa". to #746 (1918). Scr. 1927.
1st 751-756	Hammond Car Co.	1895	Reblt. 1916 from 1000 series. Scr. 1926.
1st 757-759	United Railroads	1918	Scr. 1935 (same group as 760-771).
2nd 725-734	J.G. Brill	1913-17	Purchased 2nd hand Williamsport Ry, PA (1935) Scr. (1941)
2nd 735-736	J.G. Brill	1916	Purchased 2nd hand Williamsport Ry, PA (1936) Scr. (1945)
2nd 740-746	St. Louis Car Co.	1918	Purchased 2nd hand EStL&S (1936) Scr. (1946); #745 in 1945
747-750	St. Louis Car Co.	1918	Purchased 2nd hand EStL&S (1936) Scr. (1946); #750 in 1941.
2nd 751-759	St. Louis Car Co.	1918	Purchased 2nd hand EStL&S (1936) Scr. 1941.
760-771	United Railroads	1918	Scr. 1935, except #765 Scr. 1927.
772-778	United Railroads	1919	Scr. 1928
2nd 778	Market Str. Ry.	1923	See 2nd #1424.
779-783	Market Str. Ry.	1923	Scr. 1946.
1st 784	Market Str. Ry.	1923	To #792 (12-11-23) Scr. (1946) Also see #725-#726 above.
1st 785	Market Str. Ry	1923	To #793 (12-13-23) Scr. (1946) Also see #725-726 above.
786-836	Market Str. Ry.	1923-26	Scr. 1945-48 (#792-ex 1st #784; #793 ex 1st #785). #798 See note.
837-843	Market Str. Ry.	1925	Built as "Blue Gold" #2008-#2014. In 1927 to #837-843. Scr. 1946-48
844-922	Market Str. Ry.	1927-30	#980 destroyed by fire (3-29-45) #895 renumbered #980 same date. Scr. 1945-50.
923-941	Market Str. Ry.	1930	Scr. 1948-50
942-943	Market Str. Ry.	1930	Scr. 1948
944-988	Market Str. Ry.	1931-33	Scr. 1948-50 #974 to Bay Area Elect. Ass'n (1950) #980 des. by fire (1945).
989	Market Str. Ry.	1933	Built as first one-man; two-man car. Scr. 1949.
990-994	Market Str. Ry	1933	Scr. 1949
1225-1244	Laelede Car Co.	1903	Assigned San Mateo line before & after "Big Subs". Scr. 1948-49.
1300-1349	St. Louis Car Co.	1903-04	Scr. 1927-35. See note.
1st 1350	Press Steel Co.	1904	To #1391 by 1910. Scrapped 1930. See note.
1350-1374	St. Louis Car Co.	1904	Scr. 1927-35. See note.
1375-1424	St. Louis Car Co.	1905	Scr. 1927-35. See note.
2nd 1424	Market Str. Ry.	1923	Rebuilt standard one-man, two-man car. #778 in 1935, Scrapped 1948.
1500-1549	American Car Co.	1906	Known as the "Chicago Cars". Stored 1935. All Scr. by 1940. See note.
1550-1749	St. Louis Car Co.	1907	Scr. starting 1930 with most in 1941. See note.

Note: A number of Market Street cable cars were rebuilt after the 1906 earthquake and fire into 950, 1000, 1100 to 1215 series electric street cars, but no reliable records as to how many. All scrapped by 1920.

NOTES

101-180 class. When under Muni ownership 1944 numbers conflicted with their 100 series, so the following had their first digit changed to "4". Example: 101 to 401, others 402, 404, 405, 410-412, 424, 426, 430-433, 435, 439, 444, 450-452, 454, 457, 458, 460-462, 471-473, 480. #180 was only car in this series rebuilt to one-man car in 1935. Back to two-man when Muni took over in 1944.

201-265 class. When under Muni numbers conflicted with their 200 series, the following had their first digit change to "6". 201 to 601, others 602-613, 622, 635, 638, 644, 647,647, 651, 654, 657, 659, 660, 662, 663, 665. #265 became a one-man car in 1935. Rebuilt to two-man when Muni took over in 1944.

601-662 class. When United Railroads took over the street car system in 1902, the roster contained several hundred single truck cars. They were whittled down with 29 going to Presidio and Ferries in 1907 (19 repurchased for parts in 1923) with many others to Maintenance service cars, homes and sheds. By 1912, United Railroads selected the best of what was left and numbered them 601-662. In 1915, 14 were rebuilt for multiple use on the Fillmore counterbalance line. Six were again rebuilt for the same line in 1921. The line ended, April 5, 1941, bringing the era of the single truck car in passenger service to an end. One fully restored, #578, exists today as a Muni festival car. Another #755, later Presidio and Ferries #28, Muni #317, later service car #C-4 is derelict at the Western Railway Museum, Rio Vista. (1990).

671-680 class. Ex San Francisco and San Mateo Railway #41-50 taken over by United in 1902. The disposition of these cars was as follows: (Roster furnished by Bert Ward)

671 To Mail Car "D" 1905. Destroyed by fire 1906.
672 To Mail Car "E" 1905. Destroyed by fire 1906.
673 To Line car #0304
674 To SSFR&P #1 (1904); #44 (1908), #727 (1908).
675 To SSFR&P #2 (1904); #45 (1908), Scr. 1926
676 To Olivet Memorial Park #2 (1906)
677 To Reno Traction (1906)
678 To SSFR&P #46 (1908) Ret. to United RR. To #729 (1919) Scr. 1927.
679 To SSFR&P #47 (1908) Ret. to United RR. To #729 (1919) Scr. 1927.
680 To SSFR&P #48 (1908); #48 (1908) Ret. to United RR. To #730 (1919) Scr. 1927.

SF&SM - San Francisco & San Mateo Railway

South San Francisco Railway & Power Company.

681-698 class. Ex SF&SM #51-70. Taken over by United Railroads in 1902. #61 to Private Car "San Francisco", and #67 to Funeral Car #2. In 1907 #696 to wrecker #0507. #698 to #696 (1915) All scrapped 1926-27.

#798 Located in the Sierra foothills the shell sans trucks was brought to Muni Metro yard in 1986. To restore the car to its former appearance a deal was worked out with the California Department of Corrections to have the work accomplished at thier Deul Vocational Institute near Tracy, CA. It was moved to this location in July, 1989. The car outshopped at Elkton, April 7, 1924 was retired July 5, 1946.

1300-1424 class. In 1912-1913 extensively rebuilt into PAYE cars. #1310 destroyed in fire, April 18, 1906 and #1300 took its place. #1358 account wreck and scrapped, #1374 took its place. 1st #1424 to 2nd #1374. #1391 wrecked and scrapped and 1st #1350 (Press Steel car) to its number by 1910. All cars scrapped by January, 1936.

2nd #1424 Built by Market Street Railway, Elkton Shops (1924) for the South San Francisco line. When that line went one-man in 1934 shifted to Visitacion line and when that line went one-man in 1935 to Elkton Shops and rebuilt to 2nd #778.

1500-1549 class. Account earthquake and fire that followed, April 18, 1906, an appeal was made for immediate delivery of cars. American Car Co., had 50 ready for the Chicago City Railway, so this order was diverted to San Francisco. The cars became known as the "Chicago" cars. #1508 was demolished in a run away down hill, April 28, 1915. Completely rebuilt into a "California" type car. #1527 was renumbered #1499 for a short time in 1919 when the car struck and killed a boy and the father threatended to shoot anyone assigned to #1527. All scrapped between 1935 and 1940.

1550-1749 class. Three of this series were in bad wrecks: #1690 (1918), #1722 (1918) and #1745 (1915). Each rebuilt to "California" type cars and upgraded for operation on the San Mateo line. In 1930-31 #1690 renumbered to #1716 and#1745 to #715. #1722 retained its number. The purpose of the renumberings was to keep a sequence of car numbers assigned to the Geneva barn. When the San Francisco Municipal Railway took over in 1944, there were but nine left: #1553, 1572, 1583, 1595, 1599, 1715, 1731 (Scr. 1948) and 1716, 1722 (Scr. 1949) #1553 and #1715 were the only ones to receive the Muni cream, green and wings design.

MISCELLANEOUS CARS

1st 1	**?**	**?**	**Funeral car "Cypress Lawn". From Cypress Lawn Cemetery Ass'n, 1900. Scr. 1906.**
1st 2	**St. Louis Car Co.**	**1901**	**Ex SF&SM Ry #67. To Funeral Car #2. To Party Car "Sierra". 1908. See car "Sierra".**
2nd 1, 3, 4	**United RR**	**1903-04**	**Funeral Cars. #4 to 2nd #2 (1908). All three scrapped 1926.**
S.F.	**St. Louis Car Co.**	**1901**	**ExSF&SM Ry #61. To Party Car (1904) Sold 1948 for restaurant, El Verano, CA. Now at Bay Area Electric Museum Rio Vista (1990).**
Sierra	**United RR**	**1901**	**Reblt from Funeral Car # 2 to Party Car (1908) Idle (1915) Scr. 1927.**
Hermosa	**St. Louis Car Co.**	**1896**	**Party Car. Reblt to #746 (1919). Scr. 1927 - See 1st #746.**

...D for trip in one direction to destination in accordance with the rules of the Company, if presented at ...fer point on date of issue within the time indicated by punch mark. In case of controversy please pay ...and apply for redress at room 719 of the Company's Offices at 5? Sutter Street.

Market Street Railway Co.

RIDE ALL YOU WANT
--- SUNDAY PASS 20c ---

THIS TRANSFER IS NOT TRANSFERABLE AND NOT A STOP-OVER PRIVILEGE.

Vol. I SEPTEMBER, 1939 No. 1

Traffic in Downtown Area Presents Real Problem

Every progressive city in the United States has been or is now faced with a traffic problem. The very fact that a city is progressive means that more and more vehicles seek the use of its streets. Ways and means must be found to relieve traffic congestion in order that cities may grow and prosper. San Francisco is no exception. It has not to date solved its traffic problem.

It is our humble opinion that a few sim... changes c... be made immediat... alleviate t...

MOTORMAN'S POCKET BULLETIN

No. 7

Since the Profit-Sharing Plan went into effect we have received many requests from platform men for suggestions showing how to cut down the waste in operation,—particularly for ideas on HOW TO STOP THE WASTE OF ELECTRICAL ENERGY.

You may remember that in 1929 the "Five-point rule" together with Motorman's bulletins telling how to save power resulted in a saving ... $26,000 for the year. Some of this ...iles;—but at ...7,000 or $18,- ...

... carelessness ...;—" also an ...ING HABITS ...

...OUR OWN IN- ...Profit through ...gestions which ...ears ago.

...060,535. Some- ...y is an amount ...wasted through ...PAYS FOR that ...R IS PAID FOR

CITY WIDE SERVICE BY WHITE FRONT CARS

MARKET STREET RAILWAY CO.
San Francisco

San Francisco

A GUIDE OF THE CITY WIDE SYSTEM

NUMBERED GREEN CARS AND COACHES WITH White fronts

RAIL AND RUBBER TIRED VEHICLES OF TRANSPORTATION

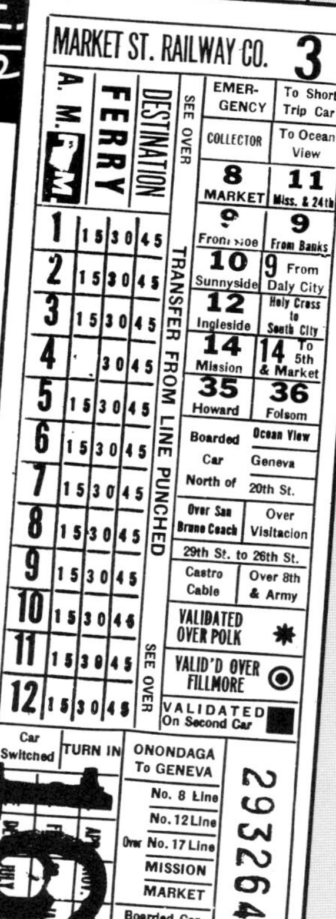

United Railroads of San Francisco.

OBSERVATION CAR "GOLDEN GATE."

Observation Cars in charge of competent guides leave Market, Post and Montgomery Streets, and Market and Second Streets, at 10 A. M. and 2 P. M. daily, Sundays included; returning at 1.30 P. M. and 5.30 P. M.

**See Union Square, City Hall,
Lick Monument, Mechanics Pavilion,
St. Ignatius Church and College,
New Post Office, U. S. Mint, Southern Pacific Hospital,
Mission Dolores, Affiliated Colleges,
Cliff House, Ocean Beach, Etc., Etc.**

Distance, Round Trip, 20 Miles.

THE NEW OBSERVATION CAR "CALIFORNIA."

Board one of these cars and see San Francisco. The only trip of its kind. Passing every principal point of interest.

**COMPETENT GUIDES IN CHARGE. - - -
PARTICULARLY DESIGNED FOR TOURISTS.**

An instructive, pleasant ride aboard a comfortable and well-equipped car.

SEE FRONT PAGE FOR PARTICULARS.

Distance, Round Trip, 20 miles.

THE PARLOR CAR "HERMOSA."

Handsomely upholstered. Beautifully furnished, seating 30 persons. May be chartered as a party car, at the following rates:

Within City Limits,		
During the day,	- - -	*$2.50 per hour.*
Minimum charge,	-	*$10.00*
Evenings, 7 P. M. to 1 A. M.,	- - -	*$12.00*

This Company is prepared to furnish other cars at reasonable rates.

UNITED RAILROADS OF SAN FRANCISCO,

ROOM 822 RIALTO BUILDING,
NEW MONTGOMERY AND MISSION STS.
SAN FRANCISCO, CAL.

G. F. CHAPMAN,
GENERAL MANAGER.

SUBURBAN CAR.

These cars are operated from Fifth and Market sts. direct to San Mateo, passing through Ocean View, Colma, Holy Cross, San Bruno, Tanforan, Millbrae, and Burlingame. Fare (one way), 25 cents. Cars leave as follows:

FROM FIFTH AND MARKET STS., every half hour, commencing at 6 A. M., up to 6.30 P. M., and thereafter at 7.30, 8.30, 9.30, 10.30 and 11.30 P. M.

CARS LEAVE SAN MATEO every half hour after 5.30 A. M. until 7.30 P. M., and thereafter at 8, 9, 10, 11, and 12 P. M. ON SUNDAYS cars leave every 15 minutes between 9 A. M. and 7 P. M.

MARKET STREET RAILWAY ELECTRIC STREET CARS
(United Railroads Roster)

Scr. - Scrapped Reblt - Rebuilt EStL&S - East St. Louis & Suburban Railway.

Numbers	Builder	Date	Remarks - Disposition
1- 12	St. Louis Car Co.	1906	Known as "Big Subs." Used on San Mateo line. Scr. 1933-35.
45		1900	See 671-680 note.
101-180	Jewett Car Co.	1911	#123 wrecked August 30, 1942 and Scr. All other Scr. by 1949. See Note.
201-265	American Car. Co.	1913	Known as "California" type. Scr. between 1947-50. See note
266-285	United Railroads	1920-21	#285 reblt to one-man car (1932) Back to two man (1939) All scr. 1945-49
286-298	Market St. Ry.	1924-25	Scr. 1945-49.
299-305	Market St. Ry.	1925	Built as "Blue Gold" cars #2001-#2007. To #299-305 (1926) Scr. 1946-48.
401	United Railroads	1914	Experimental. Ex #301. To #401 (1925) Storage (1935) Scr. 1941.
402-406	St. Louis Car Co.	1927	Purchased from EStL&S (1936). Known as Rail Sedans. Stored (1939) Scr. (1941).
407-410	St. Louis Car Co.	1924	Purchased from SStL&S (1936). Stored (1939). Scr. (1941).
601-605	Hammond Car Co.	1895	Single Truck. Reblt. one-man car United RR (1914-15). Scr. (1935) See Note.
606-612	Hammond Car Co.	1893	Single Truck. Some Reblt. One-man car. United RR (1914-15) Scr. by 1930. See Note.
617-620	Holman Car Co.	1896	Single Truck. Scr. by 1930. See note.
621-627	Hammond Car Co.	1895	Single Truck. Reblt United RR for Fillmore Hill Service. Scr. (1941) See note.
628-662	Hammond Car Co.	1895	Some reblt. by United RR (1915) All Scr. by 1935. See note.
671-680	Hammond Car Co.	1900	Ex San Francisco & San Mateo Ry #41-50. See note.
681-698	St. Louis Car Co.	1900	Ex San Francisco & San Mateo Ry #51-70. Scr. by 1927. See note.
2nd 698	Market Str. Ry.	1900	Ex Sightseeing car "City of Atlanta". Renamed "Golden Gate". Passenger car #698 (1918) Scr. 1925.
699	United Railroads	1904	Ex Sightseeing car "California". Passenger car (1918) Scr. 1925.
701-724	United Railroads	1911-12	Scr. by 1935
1st 725-726	Hammond Car Co.	1895	From #1023 & #1024 reblt to 2nd #784 and 2nd #785 (1923). Scr. 1946
1st 727-730	Hammond Car Co.	1900	See #671-680 above (Scr. 1927)
1st 731-745	Holman Car Co.	1897	Ex Sutro RR. To Sutter Str. Ry (1900); To United (1902) Scr. mid-1920s.
1st 746	St. Louis Car Co.	1896	Ex Private Car "Hermosa". to #746 (1918). Scr. 1927.
1st 751-756	Hammond Car Co.	1895	Reblt. 1916 from 1000 series. Scr. 1926.
1st 757-759	United Railroads	1918	Scr. 1935 (same group as 760-771).
2nd 725-734	J.G. Brill	1913-17	Purchased 2nd hand Williamsport Ry, PA (1935) Scr. (1941)
2nd 735-736	J.G. Brill	1916	Purchased 2nd hand Williamsport Ry, PA (1936) Scr. (1945)
2nd 740-746	St. Louis Car Co.	1918	Purchased 2nd hand EStL&S (1936) Scr. (1946); #745 in 1945
747-750	St. Louis Car Co.	1918	Purchased 2nd hand EStL&S (1936) Scr. (1946); #750 in 1941.
2nd 751-759	St. Louis Car Co.	1918	Purchased 2nd hand EStL&S (1936) Scr. 1941.
760-771	United Railroads	1918	Scr. 1935, except #765 Scr. 1927.
772-778	United Railroads	1919	Scr. 1928
2nd 778	Market Str. Ry.	1923	See 2nd #1424.
779-783	Market Str. Ry.	1923	Scr. 1946.
1st 784	Market Str. Ry.	1923	To #792 (12-11-23) Scr. (1946) Also see #725-#726 above.
1st 785	Market Str. Ry	1923	To #793 (12-13-23) Scr. (1946) Also see #725-726 above.
786-836	Market Str. Ry.	1923-26	Scr. 1945-48 (#792-ex 1st #784; #793 ex 1st #785). #798 See note.
837-843	Market Str. Ry.	1925	Built as "Blue Gold" #2008-#2014. In 1927 to #837-843. Scr. 1946-48
844-922	Market Str. Ry.	1927-30	#980 destroyed by fire (3-29-45) #895 renumbered #980 same date. Scr. 1945-50.
923-941	Market Str. Ry.	1930	Scr. 1948-50
942-943	Market Str. Ry.	1930	Scr. 1948
944-988	Market Str. Ry.	1931-33	Scr. 1948-50 #974 to Bay Area Elect. Ass'n (1950) #980 des. by fire (1945).
989	Market Str. Ry.	1933	Built as first one-man; two-man car. Scr. 1949.
990-994	Market Str. Ry	1933	Scr. 1949
1225-1244	Laelede Car Co.	1903	Assigned San Mateo line before & after "Big Subs". Scr. 1948-49.
1300-1349	St. Louis Car Co.	1903-04	Scr. 1927-35. See note.
1st 1350	Press Steel Co.	1904	To #1391 by 1910. Scrapped 1930. See note.
1350-1374	St. Louis Car Co.	1904	Scr. 1927-35. See note.
1375-1424	St. Louis Car Co.	1905	Scr. 1927-35. See note.
2nd 1424	Market Str. Ry.	1923	Rebuilt standard one-man, two-man car. #778 in 1935, Scrapped 1948.
1500-1549	American Car Co.	1906	Known as the "Chicago Cars". Stored 1935. All Scr. by 1940. See note.
1550-1749	St. Louis Car Co.	1907	Scr. starting 1930 with most in 1941. See note.

Note: A number of Market Street cable cars were rebuilt after the 1906 earthquake and fire into 950, 1000, 1100 to 1215 series electric street cars, but no reliable records as to how many. All scrapped by 1920.

NOTES

101-180 class. When under Muni ownership 1944 numbers conflicted with their 100 series, so the following had their first digit changed to "4". Example: 101 to 401, others 402, 404, 405, 410-412, 424, 426, 430-433, 435, 439, 444, 450-452, 454, 457, 458, 460-462, 471-473, 480. #180 was only car in this series rebuilt to one-man car in 1935. Back to two-man when Muni took over in 1944.

201-265 class. When under Muni numbers conflicted with their 200 series, the following had their first digit change to "6". 201 to 601, others 602-613, 622, 635, 638, 644, 647,647, 651, 654, 657, 659, 660, 662, 663, 665. #265 became a one-man car in 1935. Rebuilt to two-man when Muni took over in 1944.

601-662 class. When United Railroads took over the street car system in 1902, the roster contained several hundred single truck cars. They were whittled down with 29 going to Presidio and Ferries in 1907 (19 repurchased for parts in 1923) with many others to Maintenance service cars, homes and sheds. By 1912, United Railroads selected the best of what was left and numbered them 601-662. In 1915, 14 were rebuilt for multiple use on the Fillmore counterbalance line. Six were again rebuilt for the same line in 1921. The line ended, April 5, 1941, bringing the era of the single truck car in passenger service to an end. One fully restored, #578, exists today as a Muni festival car. Another #755, later Presidio and Ferries #28, Muni #317, later service car #C-4 is derelict at the Western Railway Museum, Rio Vista. (1990).

671-680 class. Ex San Francisco and San Mateo Railway #41-50 taken over by United in 1902. The disposition of these cars was as follows: (Roster furnished by Bert Ward)

671 To Mail Car "D" 1905. Destroyed by fire 1906.
672 To Mail Car "E" 1905. Destroyed by fire 1906.
673 To Line car #0304
674 To SSFR&P #1 (1904); #44 (1908), #727 (1908).
675 To SSFR&P #2 (1904); #45 (1908), Scr. 1926
676 To Olivet Memorial Park #2 (1906)
677 To Reno Traction (1906)
678 To SSFR&P #46 (1908) Ret. to United RR. To #729 (1919) Scr. 1927.
679 To SSFR&P #47 (1908) Ret. to United RR. To #729 (1919) Scr. 1927.
680 To SSFR&P #48 (1908); #48 (1908) Ret. to United RR. To #730 (1919) Scr. 1927.

SF&SM - San Francisco & San Mateo Railway

South San Francisco Railway & Power Company.

681-698 class. Ex SF&SM #51-70. Taken over by United Railroads in 1902. #61 to Private Car "San Francisco", and #67 to Funeral Car #2. In 1907 #696 to wrecker #0507. #698 to #696 (1915) All scrapped 1926-27.

#798 Located in the Sierra foothills the shell sans trucks was brought to Muni Metro yard in 1986. To restore the car to its former appearance a deal was worked out with the California Department of Corrections to have the work accomplished at thier Deul Vocational Institute near Tracy, CA. It was moved to this location in July, 1989. The car outshopped at Elkton, April 7, 1924 was retired July 5, 1946.

1300-1424 class. In 1912-1913 extensively rebuilt into PAYE cars. #1310 destroyed in fire, April 18, 1906 and #1300 took its place. #1358 account wreck and scrapped, #1374 took its place. 1st #1424 to 2nd #1374. #1391 wrecked and scrapped and 1st #1350 (Press Steel car) to its number by 1910. All cars scrapped by January, 1936.

2nd #1424 Built by Market Street Railway, Elkton Shops (1924) for the South San Francisco line. When that line went one-man in 1934 shifted to Visitacion line and when that line went one-man in 1935 to Elkton Shops and rebuilt to 2nd #778.

1500-1549 class. Account earthquake and fire that followed, April 18, 1906, an appeal was made for immediate delivery of cars. American Car Co., had 50 ready for the Chicago City Railway, so this order was diverted to San Francisco. The cars became known as the "Chicago" cars. #1508 was demolished in a run away down hill, April 28, 1915. Completely rebuilt into a "California" type car. #1527 was renumbered #1499 for a short time in 1919 when the car struck and killed a boy and the father threatended to shoot anyone assigned to #1527. All scrapped between 1935 and 1940.

1550-1749 class. Three of this series were in bad wrecks: #1690 (1918), #1722 (1918) and #1745 (1915). Each rebuilt to "California" type cars and upgraded for operation on the San Mateo line. In 1930-31 #1690 renumbered to #1716 and#1745 to #715. #1722 retained its number. The purpose of the renumberings was to keep a sequence of car numbers assigned to the Geneva barn. When the San Francisco Municipal Railway took over in 1944, there were but nine left: #1553, 1572, 1583, 1595, 1599, 1715, 1731 (Scr. 1948) and 1716, 1722 (Scr. 1949) #1553 and #1715 were the only ones to receive the Muni cream, green and wings design.

MISCELLANEOUS CARS

1st 1	**?**	**?**	**Funeral car "Cypress Lawn". From Cypress Lawn Cemetery Ass'n, 1900. Scr. 1906.**
1st 2	**St. Louis Car Co.**	**1901**	**Ex SF&SM Ry #67. To Funeral Car #2. To Party Car "Sierra". 1908. See car "Sierra".**
2nd 1, 3, 4	**United RR**	**1903-04**	**Funeral Cars. #4 to 2nd #2 (1908). All three scrapped 1926.**
S.F.	**St. Louis Car Co.**	**1901**	**ExSF&SM Ry #61. To Party Car (1904) Sold 1948 for restaurant, El Verano, CA. Now at Bay Area Electric Museum Rio Vista (1990).**
Sierra	**United RR**	**1901**	**Reblt from Funeral Car # 2 to Party Car (1908) Idle (1915) Scr. 1927.**
Hermosa	**St. Louis Car Co.**	**1896**	**Party Car. Reblt to #746 (1919). Scr. 1927 - See 1st #746.**

D for trip in one direction to destination in accordance with the rules of the Company, if presented at
fer point on date of issue within the time indicated by punch mark. In case of controversy please pay
and apply for redress at room 719 of the Company's Offices at 58 Sutter Street.
Market Street Railway Co.

RIDE ALL YOU WANT
--- SUNDAY PASS 20c ---

THIS TRANSFER IS NOT TRANSFERABLE AND NOT A STOP-OVER PRIVILEGE.

Vol I — SEPTEMBER, 1939 — No. 1

Traffic in Downtown Area Presents Real Problem

Every progressive city in the United States has been or is now faced with a traffic problem. The very fact that a city is progressive means that more and more vehicles seek the use of its streets. Ways and means must be found to relieve traffic congestion in order that cities may grow and prosper. San Francisco is no exception. It has not to date solved its traffic problem.

It is our humble opinion that a few sim... changes co... alleviate t... be made immediat...

MOTORMAN'S POCKET BULLETIN

No. 7

Since the Profit-Sharing Plan went into effect we have received many requests from platform men for suggestions showing how to cut down the waste in operation,—particularly for ideas on HOW TO STOP THE WASTE OF ELECTRICAL ENERGY.

You may remember that in 1929 the "Five-point rule" together with Motorman's bulletins telling how to save power resulted in a saving ... $26,000 for the year. Some of this ...iles;—but at ...7,000 or $18,- ...

...g carelessness ...c;—" also an ...TING HABITS ...

...OUR OWN IN... Profit through ...gestions which ...years ago.

...,060,535. Some...y is an amount ...wasted through ...PAYS FOR that ...R IS PAID FOR

CITY WIDE SERVICE BY WHITE FRONT CARS

MARKET STREET RAILWAY CO.
San Francisco

RAIL AND RUBBER TIRED VEHICLES OF TRANSPORTATION

CHAPTER 3

MARKET STREET RAILWAY CO. - (UNITED RAILROADS)

ROUTES

At the peak of the Market Street Railway, the system had thirty-nine numbered routes; 1-12, 14-36, 40-43 and seven un-numbered lines. The lines are listed herewith in numerical order from the inner terminal to the outer terminal and mileage of the route (1931). The compilation gives the day the electric street cars commenced operation, changes, and their final day of operation. In most cases motor buses took their place.

You will note that many car lines had their inner terminal designated as "Ferries," so named for the many ferry boat lanes that converged at the San Francisco Ferry Building docking slips from the many points across San Francisco Bay and one from Vallejo on San Pablo Bay. The heyday was in the late 1920s when 47 million commuters and main line passengers poured through the Ferry Building in a single year. To serve this mass were 32 separate street car lines (22 Market Street Railway and 10 Municipal) that came into three separate terminals at the Ferry Building: The Ferry loop for cars on Market Street, the north end stub of three tracks for lines 16 and Muni "E", and the south end stub with four tracks for cars off Mission and Howard Streets as they turned into The Embarcadero. When the Golden Gate Bridge opened in 1937 and suburban train service began on the San Francisco-Oakland Bay Bridge in 1939 to the East Bay Terminal at First & Mission Streets, the era of the ferry boat declined rapidly and ended completely with only a one-boat schedule left to Oakland Pier in 1958. Half of the street cars on Market Street lines changed their inner terminus to the East Bay Terminal in 1939, but those on the heavily travelled Mission Street continued to the Ferries until the end of street cars on Mission Street, January 15, 1949.

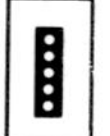

SUTTER-CALIFORNIA
(Ferry Loop to 48th and Point Lobos Ave. via Land's End)

From Ferry up Market Street to Sutter, Presidio, California, 6th Ave., Clement, 33rd Ave., private right-of-way around Land's End to Point Lobos Station. 7.75 miles. (1920)

Starts from Presidio & Sutter to Point Lobos Station. .... May 26, 1905
Line extended on Sutter to Market and outside track to Ferry loop. .... July 4, 1906
Cut back from Ferry to Sutter & Sansome account franchise dispute. Horse car takes over disputed portion .... June 1, 1908
Dispute settled. Horse car ended, street car returns to Ferry terminus .... June 3, 1913
Franchise on California between 6th & 33rd Ave. taken over by City. Line diverted one block at 6th to Clement, to 33rd, to right-of-way .... September 5, 1914
Slide at Land's End ends this portion. Line terminates at 33rd & Clement .... February 7, 1925
San Francisco Municipal Railway takes over .... September 29, 1944
Outer terminal extended from 33rd & Clement to Geary, 48th, Point Lobos, right-of-way to Sutro Baths Terminal .... November 5, 1945
Outer terminal cut back to 45th & Geary February24, 1947
Last day of street car operation .... July 2, 1949

Car #257 at Route #1 terminal at Point Lobos Station, 48th Avenue and Point Lobos Street September 19, 1913. Tracks were later extended to curve into #2 tracks so that #1 cars could go to the popular Sutro Baths and Cliff House on Sundays and holidays. ***Bob Stein collection.***

Magnificent view of the Golden Gate was seen as street car #218 on the #1 line travelled along the area known as Land's End, May 8, 1923. The Golden Gate Bridge would be in place 14 years later. On February 7, 1925, a large slide ended the scenic Land's End portion of the #1 route and the outer terminal was cut back to 33rd and Clement. ***Muni collection.***

SUTTER-CLEMENT
(Ferry Loop to Sutro Baths Terminal)

From Ferry up Market Street to Sutter, Presidio, California, Parker, Euclid, Arguello, Clement, 33rd Ave., Geary, 48th Ave. thence private right-of-way to Sutro Baths Terminal. 7.39 miles.

Commenced operation as Sutro Railroad from Presidio & Sutter to Sutro Baths. .... February 1, 1896
Taken over by United Railraods .... March 18, 1902
Extended on Sutter to Market and outside track to Ferry. (old cable line) .... July 4, 1906
History to Ferry same as #1 line
Inner terminal changed to East Bay Terminal .... January 15, 1939
San Francisco Municipal Railway takes over .... September 29, 1944
Sutro Baths terminal destroyed by fire. Cut back to 45th & Geary .... February 12, 1949
Last day of street car operation .... July 2, 1949

(Above) Car #261 at Sutro Baths near the Cliff House, was the outer terminal of the popular #2 line. On February 12, 1949 it was destroyed by fire and the line terminated at 45th and Geary. ***Guido collection.*** **(Below) September 23, 1944, during World War II, finds car #250 heading up Geary Street near 47th. Note lady motorman.** ***Bert Ward photo.***

SUTTER-JACKSON
(Ferry Loop to California & Presidio)

From Ferry up Market Street to Sutter, Fillmore, Jackson, Presidio to California. 3.78 miles.

Start of street car line .... July 4, 1906
History to Ferry same as #1 line.
San Francisco Municipal Railway takes over. .... September 29, 1944
Outer terminal changed to Sutter & Fillmore .... August 1, 1948
Last day of street car operation .... July 2, 1949

At Jackson and Steiner in the year 1948, note the cable car tracks, which in this period was the outer turing point for the Powell-Jackson-Washington cable line. ***Tom Gray photo.***

TURK-EDDY (EARLIER ROUTE)
(Ferry Loop to 6th Ave. & Fulton)

From Ferry up Market Street to Eddy (Turk inbound), Divisadero, Sacramento, Arguello, Lake, 6th Ave., Clement, 8th Ave., loop to Fulton return on 6th Ave. 5.82 miles.

Start of street car line . . . . *February 1, 1897*
#31 line takes over Turk & Eddy portion . . . . *May 15, 1932*
Old route remains in Owl service to ——— . . . . *June 16, 1935*

SUTTER-SACRAMENTO (LATER ROUTE)
(Ferry Loop to 6th Ave. & Fulton)

From Ferry up Market Street to Sutter, Fillmore, Sacramento, Arguello, Lake, 6th Ave., Clement, 8th Ave., loop to Fulton return on 6th Ave. 5.00 miles.

New route starts . . . . *June 16, 1935*
Inner terminal changed to East Bay Terminal . . . . *January 15, 1939*
San Francisco Municipal Railway takes over . . . . *September 29, 1944*
Last day of street car operation . . . . *July 31, 1948*

Car #244 at the outer terminal at 6th and Fulton, May 1940. ***Bert Ward photo.***

McALLISTER
(Ferry Loop to beach at La Playa & Balboa)

From Ferry up Market Street to McAllister, private right-of-way between Central & Masonic, to Fulton, La Playa to Balboa loop. 7.08 miles.

From Ferry to 24th & Fulton (replaced cable line)	*August 12, 1906*
Extended from 24th & Fulton to Balboa loop at Ocean Beach	*March 13, 1911*
Inner terminal changed to East Bay Terminal	*January 15, 1939*
San Francisco Municipal Railway takes over	*September 29, 1944*
Inner terminal to McAllister-Jones-Market	*March 15, 1948*
Last day of street car operation	*June 5, 1948*

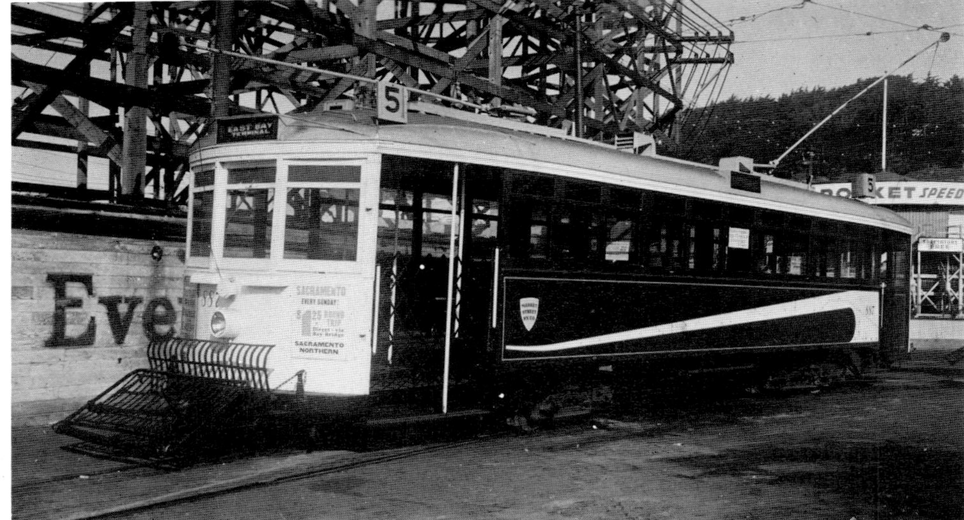

(Right) In 1939 car #887 sports the new white flourish decor at the Ocean Beach terminal. What is interesting is the dash sign, advertising Sacramento Northern's $1.25 roundtrip fare San Francisco to Sacramento every Sunday. *Guido collection.* **(Below) Car #887 inbound on Fulton at Park Presidio.** *Will Whittaker photo.*

(Above) "Chicago" car #1509 stops at loading zone between 3rd and 4th Streets on Market before heading to McAllister Street turnoff with destination Playland-at-the Beach. *Tom Gray photo.* (Below) Street cars were near the end of the line when this photo was taken of car #696 in June 1948. *Art Lloyd photo.*

HAIGHT-MASONIC
(Ferry Loop to 9th Ave. & Pacheco)

From Ferry up Market Street to Haight, Masonic, Frederick, Clayton, Carl, Stanyan, Parnassus, Judah, 9th Ave. to Pacheco. 5.81 miles.

Starts from Ferry on Market to Hayes, Fillmore, Oak, Masonic, Frederick, Clayton, Carl, Stanyan, Parnassus to 3rd Ave. Known as Hayes-Masonic line .... *June 10, 1906*
Route change with extension from 3rd Ave. to 9th Ave. to Pacheco .... *June 15, 1912*
New line established going out Haight to Masonic eliminating Fillmore & Oak .... *February 7, 1916*
San Francisco Municipal Railway takes over .... *September 29, 1944*
Last day of street car operation .... *July 3, 1948*

(Above) Jewett car #160 makes the Ferry Loop during the Golden Gate International Exposition held on man-made Treasure Island in San Francisco Bay, 1939-1940. *Waldemar Sievers photo, Harre Demoro collection.* **(Right) Car #147 swings into the Ferry Loop in July 1948. Today (1990) the street car, tracks and all buildings in the background are gone.** *Fred Matthews, Jr., photo.*

HAIGHT-OCEAN
(Ferry Loop to La Playa & Balboa)

From Ferry Loop up Market Street to Haight, Stanyan, Frederick, Lincoln Way, private right-of-way to La Playa & Balboa. (7.96 miles)

Old cable line. Starts as street car line Ferry to Haight & Stanyan .... December 26, 1906
Takes over former No. 20 line. Extended on Stanyan from Haight to Frederick, Lincoln Way, private right-of-way across Golden Gate Park to La Playa & Balboa .... February 7, 1916
Inner terminal changed to East Bay Terminal .... January 15, 1939
San Francisco Municipal Railway takes over. .... September 29, 1944
Outer terminal cut back to 47th Ave. & Lincoln Way .... February 23, 1947
Last day of street car operation .... July 3, 1948

(Above) Car #152 ambles along Lincoln Way near 2nd Avenue, April 6, 1938. ***Will Whittaker photo.*** **(Left) on the only right-of-way allowed across Golden Gate Park, car #146 emerges from a roadway overpass as it travels between Lincoln Way and Fulton, thence to Playland-at-the-Beach, the line's outer terminal.** ***Guido collection.***

MARKET-CASTRO
(Ferry Loop to Castro & 18th Street)

From Ferry Loop up to Market Street to Castro to 18th Street. (3.33 miles)

Replaced cable line. Starts as street car line (cable car remains 18th to 26th) .... Late 1906
(Rush hour service on 18th to Danvers Street)
San Francisco Municipal Railway takes over .... September 29, 1944
Line discontinued .... December 17, 1944
Line resumed .... November 5, 1945
Line from Castro & Market to 18th Street discontinued .... June 26, 1947
New outer terminal through Twin Peaks Tunnel to West Portal & Ulloa .... June 27, 1947
Last day of street car operation .... July 1, 1947

(Above) During peak hours the #8 line operated to 18th and Danvers as its outer terminus. ***Will Whittaker photo.*** **(Below) This scene only took place four days, June 27-July 1, 1947. Because of construction work #8 cars had their outer terminal changed to West Portal and Ulloa on the other side of the Twin Peaks tunnel. Only Muni cars were used, as attested by this photo. July 1, 1947 was the last day for street cars on this line.** ***Art Lloyd photo.***

VALENCIA
(This line had the distinction of having four outer terminals)
(Ferry Loop to 29th & Noe)
(Ferry Loop to Cortland & Banks)
(Ferry Loop to Richland & Andover)
(Ferry Loop to Daly City, San Jose & Mission)

From Ferry up Market Street to Valencia, Mission, 29th Street to Noe. 4.78 miles.

Replaced cable line to 29th. Starts as street car operation to 29th & Noe	*November 1, 1906*
Added line out Mission to Cortland to Banks replacing #24 line	June 16, 1935
Added line out Mission to Richland to Andover replacing #23 line	April 16, 1938
Added line 29th to Guerrero, 30th, Chenery, San Jose to Daly City, Replaced #26 line	June 13, 1939
From 29th to Daly City discontinued	November 5, 1939
29th & Noe and Cortland lines diverted to East Bay Terminal	January 15, 1939
San Francisco Municipal Railway takes over	September 29, 1944
Inner terminal diverted from Market to 14th, Mission to Ferry - all three lines	February 4, 1945
Cortland line ends	December 16, 1946
Richland line outer terminal cut back to Leese Street	December 16, 1946
Richland line extended back to Murray Street	May 21, 1947
Last day of street car operation remaining two lines	January 15, 1949

(Left) Car #1580 swings into Valencia Street from Market heading for 29th and Noe Streets. *Tom Gray photo.* (Below) From the period March 27 to November 11, 1946, due to sewer work on Muni's "J" line, the "J" took over the #9 line from Market to 29th and Noe Streets, Muni #94, the only Muni car to receive the small "V" on its end is photographed at 29th and Noe Street *Bert Ward photo.*

(Above) The #9 line had four terminals at one time. Car #1575 is heading out on one of them, which had its terminus at Banks and Courtland. Photo at 29th and Mission. *Tom Gray photo.* (Left) Another section of the #9 line went out Richland Avenue. Photo taken February 1944 at Marcy Place and Richland. *Will Whittaker photo.* (Below) The longest section of the #9 line. Outer terminal at Mission and San Jose Avenue. (formerly #26 line). Car #919 inbound having just crossed the old Southern Pacific Colma line at Sunnyside (Monterey Blvd.) and San Jose Avenue. *Waldemar Sievers photo, Harre Demoro collection.*

SUNNYSIDE
(Ferries to Monterey Blvd. & Gennessee Street)

From Ferries on Embarcadero to Mission, 14th, Guerrero, San Jose Ave., 30th, Chenery, Diamond, Monterey Blvd. (former name Sunnyside) to Gennessee Street. 6.50 miles.

Start of street car operation .... *Prior 1915*
Last day of street car operation .... *January 27, 1940*

Car #802 passes underneath old Southern Pacific Colma line trestle on Guerrero between 25th and 26th Street. *Guido collection.*

MISSION-24TH STREET
(Ferries to 24th & Hoffman Streets)

From Ferries on Embarcadero to Mission, to 22nd, Chattanooga, 24th to Hoffman Ave. Return 24th, Dolores, then 22nd. 4.79 miles.

Start of street car operation .... *May 5, 1906*
San Francisco Municipal Railway takes over .... *September 29, 1944*
Last day of street car operation .... *January 15, 1949*

Car #284 at end of line at 24th and Hoffman, May 28, 1943. *Will Whittaker photo.*

MISSION & INGLESIDE
(Ferries to Sloat Blvd. & Great Highway)

From Ferries on Embarcadero to Mission, Onondaga, Ocean, Junipero Serra, Sloat Blvd. to Great Highway (Ocean Beach). 10.25 miles (longest line in city)

Street car service resumed after 1906 earthquake and fire . . . . *May 6, 1906*
San Francisco Municipal Railway takes over . . . . *September 29, 1944*
Outer terminal cut back to Geneva & Mission . . . . *April 8, 1945*
Last day of street car operation . . . . *October 31, 1948*

(Above) Car #1725 prepares to depart from the concrete loading platforms at Fleishhacker Zoo and Ocean Beach, at the outer terminus of the #12 line. Looking east up Sloat Blvd., the Sunset District was a lonely looking location in this July 11, 1914 view. *Muni collection.* **(Below) Twenty-one years later, car #1580 is ready for its return trip over San Francisco's longest line, with departure from the Zoo and Ocean. (After the crew has finished their 10 cent hamburger or hot dog?)** *Guido collection.*

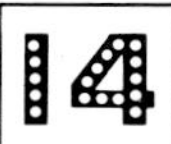

MISSION-CEMETERIES
(Ferries to Daly City to Holy Cross)

From Ferries on Embarcadero to Mission to Daly City. (Holy Cross on certain holidays and Sundays) 7.83 miles.

Street car service resumed after 1906 earthquake and fire .... *May 6, 1906*
San Francisco Municipal Railway takes over .... *September 29, 1944*
Last day of street car operation .... *January 15, 1949*

(Left) Car #278 rolls past Highland Avenue on Mission Street during World War II period, March 16, 1944. *Will Whitaker photo.* (Below) Car #1722 under Muni ownership outbound on Mission at Steuart, July 1948. Note Audiffred Building in background. Built in 1889 by Hippolite d'Audiffred in 19th century French style. At one time famous waterfront saloons Bulkhead and Riordan's occupied the lower floor. The Sailor's Union of the Pacific as the International Seaman's Union also had its headquarters in this location. Well known labor leader Harry Bridges also had his office here. It survived the earthquake and fire in 1906, however, it was completely gutted by fire in August 1979. Fortunately the exterior facade remained. The interior was rehabilitated in a splendid old-time decor. Mostly law offices occupy this historic building today (1990). *Fred H. Matthews, Jr., photo.*

KEARNY-NORTH BEACH
(3rd & Townsend S.P. Station to North Beach)

From 3rd & Townsend, Southern Pacific station, on 3rd to Kearny, Broadway, Powell to Jefferson (Piers 41-43). 2.64 miles.

Started as a street car line by old Market Street Railway	*Around 1900*
Line discontinued	*September 12, 1941*
San Francisco Municipal Railway takes over	*September 29, 1944*
Line resumed with inner terminal extended out 3rd, Mariposa, Illinois to 19th	*May 15, 1945*
Last day of street car operation	*October 7, 1946*

(Above) Car #803 ready for return trip downtown at Southern Pacific 3rd and Townsend Station during one-man car days in the year 1936. ***Guido collection.*** **(Below) Car #821 at the intersection of Kearny and Pacific heading for the SP Station and Union Iron Works, May 28, 1943. Cars assigned to this route had their cross seats removed and replaced with longitudinal seats for higher capacity during the war period.** ***Will Whittaker photo.***

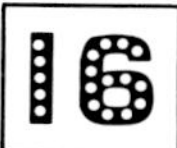

THIRD-KEARNY
(Ferries to Six Mile House (Sunnydale & Old County Road)

From Ferry Building north on Embarcadero to Broadway, Kearny, 3rd, County Road to Six Mile House at Sunnydale. 7.47 miles.

Started as a street car line by old Market Street Railway .... *Around 1900*
Last day of street car operation .... *September 12, 1941*

Car #962 crosses busy Market Street; Kearny, 3rd and Geary Streets intersection heading out 3rd Street for Visitacion Valley in mid-1930's. It was one of the longest street car routes, 7.47 miles. Notice Lotta's Fountain on the traffic island. This 24-foot fountain dates from 1875, when it was presented to San Francisco by Lotta Crabtree, a noted actress of the time. The fountain is still standing (1990), although the adjacent, unusual-style "birdcage" traffic signal is long-gone. ***Bert Ward photo.***

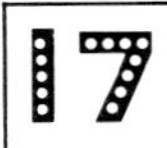

HAIGHT-INGLESIDE
(Ferries to 19th & Sloat Blvd.)

From Ferry up Market Street to Haight, Stanyan, Frederick, Lincoln Way, 20th Ave., Wawona, 19th Ave. to Sloat Blvd. 7.70 miles. (On summer Sundays used #12 line on Sloat to Ocean Beach).

Began Victoria & Ocean, Sloat, 19th, Wawona, 20th then Rte. #20 to S.P. Depot, change to above .... *February 17, 1916*
Outer terminal cut back to 19th & Wawona .... *December 29, 1937*
San Francisco Municipal Railway takes over .... *September 29, 1944*
Inner terminal changed to off Market at 12th to Mission to Ferries .... *February 4, 1945*
Last day of street car operation .... *December 21, 1945*

Before the outer terminal was moved back to 20th and Wawona from 19th and Sloat, on Sundays and holidays #17 line cars continued on Sloat Blvd. to #12's end of the line at Ocean Beach as shown in this photo. ***Will Whittaker photo.***

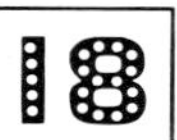

MISSION
(Fifth & Market to Daly City)

From Fifth & Market on Fifth to Mission to Daly City. 6.77 miles. To cemeteries on Holidays.

Start of street car operation .... *Prior to 1915*
Last day of street car operation *1935*
(Line was mainly a rush hour operation. 1936-37 Memorial Day only to Cemeteries)

The main purpose of this route was to serve the cemeteries on Sundays and holidays. Car #1731 at the end of the line at Holy Cross Cemetery. ***Guido collection.***

NINTH-POLK
(9th & Brannan to Polk & North Point Streets)

From 9th & Brannan, on 9th across Market to Larkin, Post, Polk to North Point Street. 2.79 miles.

Former Sutter Street RR cable line. To street car operation to Lombard Street	*Late 1906*
Extended from Lombard to North Point Street	*1915*
Line ended	*June 25, 1939*
Line resumed	*July 15, 1940*
San Francisco Municipal Railway takes over	*September 29, 1944*
Inner terminal to Hayes and Larkin	*September 29, 1944*
Last day of street car operation	*September 29, 1945*

Car #813 at 9th and Brannan terminal, July 26, 1937 when one-man operation on this line was in effect. ***Will Whittaker photo.***

EILLIS-O'FARRELL
(S.P. 3rd & Townsend Station to Golden Gate Park)

From Southern Pacific Station, 3rd & Townsend, on Townsend to 4th, across Market to Ellis, Hyde (outbound), O'Farrell, Divisadero, Oak (outbound), Page (Inbound) to Stanyan, Frederick, Lincoln Way, private right-of-way across Golden Gate Park to La Playa & Balboa. 7.69 miles.

Street car route established by Market Street Railway . . . . Prior to 1902
Outer terminal cut back to Haight & Stanyan when #7 extended to beach . . . . February 6, 1916
San Francisco Municipal Railway takes over . . . . September 29, 1944
Outer terminal cut back to Divisadero . . . . January 27, 1946
Inner terminal ended at Ellis & Market when Muni "F" extended to SP station . . . . September 8, 1947
Last day of street car operation . . . . September 27, 1947

On a cloudy morning in July 1943, car #300 swings into Hyde from Ellis Street on its outbound trip to Golden Gate Park. *Will Whittaker photo.*

HAYES
(Ferry Loop to Hayes & Stanyan)

From Ferry up Market Street to Hayes, Fillmore, Oak, Masonic, Frederick, Clayton, Carl, Stanyan, Parnassus to 3rd Ave.

Old cable car line. Start of electric street car service . . . . June 10, 1906
Route changed: Ferry, Market, Hayes, Stanyan to Fulton . . . . February 7, 1916
Outer terminal extended on Fulton from Stanyan to 8th Ave. to Clement and weekends and Holidays on Fulton to La Playa & Balboa . . . . Early 1920's
Outer terminal permanent at 8th & Clement (5.24 miles) . . . . Early 1930's
San Francisco Municipal Railway takes over . . . . September 29, 1944
Outer terminal cut back to Larkin and Hayes . . . . March 15, 1948
Last day of street car operation . . . . June 5, 1948

"Chicago" car #1522 pauses at the Ferry Loop in the year 1936 before it heads out on Market Street to its turnoff at Hayes. *Tom Gray photo.*

FILLMORE-16TH
(Bay & Fillmore to 16th & Bryant)

From Bay on Fillmore to Green then counterbalance cable for two blocks to Broadway, continue on Fillmore to Duboce, Church, 16th, Kansas, 17th, Connecticut, 18th, 3rd to Car Barn at 23rd looping through barn. 5.11 miles.

Start of street car operation (Bay & Fillmore to 16th & Bryant) 1895
United Railroads takes control .... March 8, 1902
Single truckers Bay & Fillmore to Broadway, Double truck to outer terminal 1902
Extended from 16th & Bryant to Car Barn at 3rd and 23rd .... Prior 1905
Inner terminal extended on Fillmore from Bay to Marina Blvd. .... August 29, 1925
Fillmore Hill counterbalance discontinued. Broadway end of line .... April 5, 1941
San Francisco Municipal Railway takes over .... September 29, 1944
Last day of street car operation .... July 31, 1948

(Above) Prior to 1902 single truck cars with their hooking device for the Fillmore Hill counterbalance from Broadway to Green Streets ran the complete route. After United Railroads took over in 1902 the line was split; standard cars to Broadway and Fillmore then change to counterbalance equipped cars as this photo shows. ***Will Whittaker photo.*** **(Left) On the two-block counterbalance system, one car pulls the other up, both with controls open to half power. They would pass at the center point, Vallejo Street, as shown in this photo.** ***Guido collection.***

612
BAY
AND
FILLMORE

(Left) An exceptional photo of single trucker #612 decending on left side of Fillmore Hill, August 7, 1914. Note gas lamp of the times and wooden sidewalk planks with cross cleats for firm footing. *Muni collection.*

(Above) Car #622 heading up Fillmore Hill between Vallejo and Broadway. Note direction of car is on the left side of street. The cars alternated on counterbalance position. *Will Whittaker photo.*

FILLMORE-VALENCIA
(Sacramento & Divisadero to Richland & Andover)

From Divisadero on Sacramento to Fillmore, McAllister, Gough, Market, Valencia, Mission, Richland to Andover Street. 5.08 miles.

Start of street car operation .... *September 6, 1914*
Line discontinued except shuttle on Richland between Mission/Andover .... *June 16, 1935*
Line resumed from Richland & Andover via Mission to 5th & Market .... *October 28, 1937*
Incorporated in #9 line .... *April 16, 1938*

While this line was discontinued, June 16, 1935, it was reactiviated on October 28, 1937. This photo was taken several days later car #937 passes Randall Street on Mission. A few months later, April 16, 1938. Route #23 became a part of the #9 line. *Tom Gray photo.*

MISSION-RICHMOND
(8th Ave. & Fulton to Cortland & Banks)

From Fulton on 8th Ave. to Clement, 6th Ave. Lake, Arguello, Sacramento, Divisadero, Page (Oak inbound), Fillmore, Duboce, Church, 16th, Mission, Cortland to Banks. Inbound cars arrived at terminus via 6th Ave. to Fulton, thus making a loop. 7.32 miles.

Start of street car operation with outer terminal at 29th & Mission .... *May 20, 1906*
Outer terminal extended to Cortland & Banks .... *Prior 1915*
Changed to Divisadero & Sacramento on Divisadero to Page, Page (Oak inbound), Fillmore,
Duboce, Church, 16th to Bryant. #9 line took over to Cortland & Banks .... *June 16, 1935*
Outer terminal to Page & Fillmore returning on Oak Street *1936*
Last day of street car operation .... *April 5, 1941*

Car #1334 at outer terminal, March 6, 1916. Note spelling of Divisadero in those days. ***Muni collection.***

SAN BRUNO
(5th & Market to Five Mile House (San Bruno & Wilde)

From 5th & Market on Fifth to Bryant, Army, Bayshore Blvd., San Bruno to Five Mile House at Wilde. 5.35 miles.

Start of street car operation .... *Prior 1906*
After earthquake and fire, 1906, resumed operation to Dwight & San Bruno, outer terminal with inner terminal at 26th & Folsom .... *May 1, 1906*
Inner terminal to 5th & Market .... *Prior 1914*
Outer terminal extended to Five Mile House (Wilde Ave.) .... *February 9, 1914*
Line discontinued .... *February 16, 1937*
Line resumed .... *September 8, 1942*
San Francisco Municipal Railway takes over .... *September 29, 1944*
Outer terminal extended to Arleta & Bayshore Blvd. (9/29/44), inner terminal to Ferries .... *April 9, 1945*
Outer terminal cut to Army & Potrero. Muni "H" takes over outer porion .... *December 5, 1946*
Last day of street car operation .... *July 31, 1948*

Car # 127 at the outer terminal at Wilde and San Bruno Avenue. ***Bert Ward photo.***

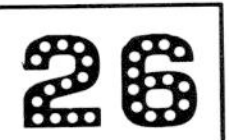

GUERRERO-DALY CITY
(Ferry Building to Daly City)

From Ferries on Embarcadero to Mission, 14th, Guerrero, 30th, Chenery, Diamond, San Jose to Mission at Daly City. (8.03 miles)

Followed portions of first electric railway (San Francisco & San Mateo Ry) *1892*
Line discontinued in favor of #9 line starting at 29th Street .... *April 16, 1938*
Resumed in part; Mission on Onondaga, Ocean, San Jose to Daly City .... *September 23, 1944*
San Francisco Municipal Railway takes over .... *September 29, 1944*
Last day of street car operation .... *February 4, 1945*

During World War II this line was resumed in part from Mission and Onondaga, Ocean, San Jose Avenue to Daly City. Car #907 at terminal point Onondaga and Mission, July 15, 1943. ***Art Lloyd photo.***

BRYANT
(2nd & Market to 26th & Mission)

From 2nd & Market, on 2nd to Bryant, 26th, to Mission. 3.89 miles

Start of street car operation .... *Prior 1915*
(1915 Guide states inbound on Bryant to 10th, Brannan, 2nd to Market)
During late 1920s and early 1930s extended from 26th & Mission to Cortland & Banks in peak hours. In 1935 outer terminal to Richland & Andover. Brannan eleminated, Bryant inbound as outbound 2nd to 26th .... *June 1937*
San Francisco Municipal Railway takes over .... *September 29, 1944*
Outbound terminal changed to 26th & Folsom via Bryant, Precita, Folsom, to 26th .... *July 11, 1948*
Last day of street car operation .... *August 13, 1948*

Ex St. Louis and Suburban Railway car #754 purchased in April 1936, pauses at 2nd and Market before taking off on its run to 26th and Mission, July 27, 1938. ***Bert Ward photo.***

FERRIES-SOUTHERN PACIFIC STATION
(Ferries to SP Third & Townsend Station)

From Ferries on Embarcadero, to Howard, Steuart, Folsom, 2nd, Brannan, 3rd to S.P. Station at Townsend. 1.47 miles. Prior to construction of the Bay Bridge the route was Ferries, Howard, Steuart, Harrison, Stanley Place, Bryant, 2nd, Brannan, 3rd to station. (Route over Rincon Hill)

Start of street car operation .... *Prior 1915*
Inner terminal to East Bay Terminal, 3rd, Brannan, 2nd Folsom, 1st, to Natoma Street .... *January 15, 1939*
Last day of street car operation .... *March 31, 1940*

This line was a connection between the Ferry Building and SP's 3rd and Townsend station. Car #750, as a one-man car ready for its run, August 18, 1938. ***Bert Ward photo.***

KEARNY-BROADWAY-SIX MILE HOUSE
(From Broadway and Davis to Six Mile House)

From Davis on Broadway to Kearny, 3rd to Wilde Ave. (Five Mile House) 6.36 miles.

Start of street car operation by old Market Street Railway . . . . *Around 1900*
Outer terminal to Six Mile House at Sunnydale . . . . *March 14, 1935*
Inner terminal changed Broadway & Davis to Sewall & Embarcadero via Kearny,
Bush to Sewall (Chestnut) & Embarcadero . . . . *September 15, 1936*
Last day of street car operation . . . . *September 12, 1941*

Car #991, as a one-man car ready for it 7½ mile run to Six Mile House at the County line in 1938. This scene is the inner terminal at Seawall (Chestnut) and Embarcadero. Note Pier 29 in the background; Belt Line roundhouse was at the right. ***Will Whittaker photo.***

ARMY STREET
(8th & Market to 22nd & Mission Streets)

From Market on 8th to Bryant, 16th, Kansas, 17th, Connecticut, 18th, 3rd, Army, Bryant, 26th, Howard, 22nd to Mission. 5.76 miles.

Start of street car operation as above . . . . *unknown*
Outer terminal cut back to 23rd & 3rd Streets . . . . *early 1930's*
Change of route: 3rd & 23rd, Army, Bryant, 26th to Mission . . . . *July 1, 1940*
Last day of street car operation . . . . *May 11, 1941*
(Reactivated during World War II for brief period)

Ex Williamsport car #734 at its outer terminal 3rd and 23rd Streets, July 12, 1935. The line served mainly the industrial area south of Market Street. ***Bert Ward photo.***

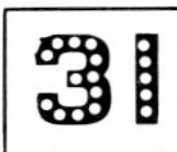

BALBOA
(Ferry Loop to Balboa & 30th)

From Ferry Loop up Market to Eddy, Divisadero, Turk, Balboa to 30th. Return on Turk, to Mason, Eddy, Market to Ferry Loop. 5.75 miles.

Start of street car operation .... May 15, 1932
San Francisco Municipal Railway takes over .... September 29, 1944
Inner terminal changed to Market & Eddy .... March 21, 1949
Last day of street car operation .... July 2, 1949

The high speed cars were assigned to the popular Balboa line as can be attested by car #979 of that class at the outer terminal at 30th and Balboa, March 13, 1939. Note brand new paint scheme. *Will Whittaker photo.*

The following lines only operated during the Panama-Pacific Golden Gate Exposition in 1915. After the Exposition was over the route numbers went to then un-numbered lines. The terminal mentioned below was located at Polk, Francisco and Van Ness area.

#32 Southern Pacific Depot-Exposition. SP Depot, 4th, Ellis, Hyde, O' Farrell, Polk to terminal.

#33 Mission-Exposition. 29th & Mission on Mission on 9th, Larkin, Post, Polk to terminal.

#34 Sutter-Exposition. Ferry Loop via Market to Sutter, Polk to terminal.

#35 Haight-Exposition. Carl & Stanyan, Clayton, Frederick, Masonic, Page (return via Oak) to Fillmore. Line lasted less than two months.

HAYES-OAK
(Ferry Loop to Stanyan & Haight)

From Ferry Loop up Market to Hayes, Fillmore, Oak (Page inbound) Stanyan to Haight. 4.10 miles.

Start of street car operation . . . . *Prior 1920*
During peak hours outer terminal 9th Ave. & Judah (Haight, Masonic, Frederick, Clayton, Carl, Stanyan, Parnassus, Judah, 9th.
Last day of street car operations *1932*

One of the St. Louis built cars (1907) heads for the Ferry Loop on Market Street in the mid-1920's. The line was discontinued in 1932. ***Tom Gray collection.***

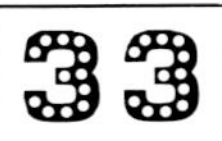

18TH AND PARK
(3rd & Harrison to Stanyan & Waller)

From 3rd on Harrison to 14th, Guerrero, 18th, Market, Clayton, Ashbury, Frederick, Clayton, Waller to Stanyan. 4.90 miles.

Start of street car operation-in part by San Francisco & San Mateo Ry *1892*
Resumed operation after 1906 earthquake and fire from
Market & Steuart, to Harrison and continue as above . . . . *May 6, 1906*
Inner terminal changed to 3rd and Harrison . . . . *Prior 1915*
Last day of street car operation . . . . *October 5, 1935*

Car #761 on Haight near Stanyan just out of Haight car house for #33 run in the year 1930. Note #33 route number on dash, a rarity. Cars (757-771) assigned to this line had longitudinal seats throughout, which fit into the line's switchback operation by not having to flip seats over on the directional change. ***Richard Schlaich collection.***

34

SIXTH & SANSOME
(Chestnut (Seawall) & Sansome to 6th & Brannan)

From Chestnut on Sansome to Bush, Kearny, Post, Taylor, 6th to Brannan. 2.83 miles.

Start of street car operation .... *Prior 1915*
Franchise on Post Street expired, so line was discontinued .... *October 1, 1936*

Platform men pose for picture at inner terminal Sansome, Chestnut (Seawall) and Embarcadero in the early 1930's. *Tom Gray collection.*

HOWARD
(Ferries to 24th & Rhode Island)

From Ferries on Embarcadero to Howard, Van Ness Ave. South, 24th to Rhode Island. 4.62 miles.

Start of street car operation .... *Prior 1915*
Franchise on Howard and Van Ness South expired. Line discontinued .... *November 5, 1939*

Car #269 has just passed under the East Bay Terminal transbay outbound trestle. Note Key System train heading toward bay bridge tracks. Year 1940. *Guido collection.*

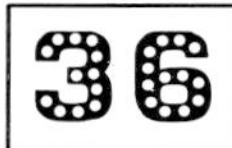

FOLSOM
(Ferries to Precita & York)

From Ferries on Embarcadero to Howard, Steuart, Folsom, Precita to York. 4.44 miles.

Start of street car operation	*Prior 1915*
Street car discontinued	*January 27, 1940*
Street cars resumed	*October 26, 1942*
San Francisco Municipal Railway takes over	*September 29, 1944*
Last day of street car operation	*January 27, 1945*

Ex St. Louis and Suburban Railway car #740 assigned to Folsom line makes a curve around Precita Park, July 1938. *Will Whittaker photo.*

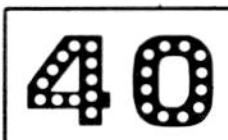

SAN MATEO INTERURBAN
(5th & Market to San Mateo Southern Pacific Station)

From Market on 5th to Mission, Daly City, Colma (private right-of-way) Holy Cross, Leipsic Jct., San Bruno, Millbrae, Burlingame, San Mateo. 19.98 miles. (Loop in San Mateo, inbound on San Mateo Drive, Baldwin, B Str., 3rd, Railroad Ave. to Station. Outbound to 2nd, B Str., Ellsworth, Popular to San Mateo Drive)

Start of street car operation .... *August 1, 1903*
Service disrupted 1906 disaster, resumed .... *May 6, 1906*
San Francisco Municipal Railway takes over .... *September 29, 1944*
Line change: Off Mission on 14th to Valencia to 28th to Mission and resume route .... *March 4, 1945*
Mission between 14th and 28th resumed .... *July 28, 1946*
Last day of street car operation .... *January 15, 1949*

(Above) "Big Sub" at Geneva car barn waiting to go on its San Mateo run in 1917. Twelve cars of this beautiful suburban type were in service on this line from 1907-1923. Being heavy power users sealed their doom. (Below) Car #1237 glides out Mission Street at South Van Ness to Daly City and right-of-way beyond to Burlingame and San Mateo in the late 1930's. *Both Tom Gray collection.*

(Top) Car #1225 gathers speed as it travels under the old SP Colma line overpass below Daly City, October 7, 1941. The structure was dismantled when SP abandoned this line; however, it soon may return when BART (Bay Area Rapid Transit) extends it tracks to the San Francisco airport. *Will Whittaker photo.* (Center) In 1947, car #1241 passes the Millbrae substation powerhouse, one of eight on the system furnishing the required 550 volts direct current (DC) to run the cars. *Guido collection.* (Right) Sturdy car #1234 sporting Muni blue and yellow decor with a "V" front is an extra for Tanforan horse racing patrons, this day in 1946. *Tom Gray photo.*

(Top) Rebuilt car #1715 with newly painted Muni green and cream with wings design is lined up awaiting the end of races atTanforan. Other cars rebuilt from accidents and served on this line were #1716 and #1722. Over 50 Market cars received the green, cream and wings design. *Tom Gray collection.* (Center) Out in the country. The stop at Millbrae Highlands, more appropriatel should have been called Millbrae Flatlands. Car #1227 gathers speed northbound along the open stretch of right-of-way. Today (1990) homes and light industry cover the area. *Guido collection.* (Bottom) Car #1242 on the streets of San Mateo on the last day of operation, January 15, 1949.

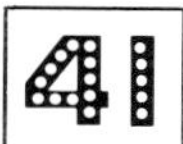

SECOND & MARKET - S.P. STATION
(2nd & Market to 3rd & Townsend S.P. Station)

From Market on 2nd to Brannan, 3rd to S.P. Station. 1.01 miles. (Commuter line)

Start of street car operation. (Peak hour service only) .... February 16, 1927
San Francisco Municipal Railway takes over .... September 29, 1944
Line discontinued when Muni "F" line took over .... January 15, 1949

On a rainy morning, June 10, 1937, car awaits the arrival of commuters at the 3rd and Townsend station. Note large route number on side of car for easy guidance. ***Will Whittaker photo.***

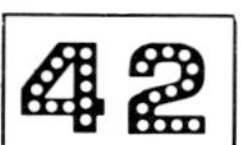

CALIFORNIA & BATTERY - S.P. STATION
(Battery & California to S.P. Station)

From California on Battery, across Market, 1st, Folsom, 2nd, Brannan, 3rd to Townsend (S.P. Station). 1.21 miles.

Start of street car operation .... Early 1930's
Line change: On Sansome from Chestnut to Bush, Kearny, 3rd to S.P. Station 1938
Last day of street car operation .... May 12, 1941

At Battery and California car #822 is ready for its run to SP's 3rd and Townsend station with evening commuters. July 1937. ***Will Whittaker photo.***

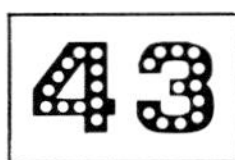

KEARNY & BROADWAY - S.P. STATION
(Kearny & Broadway to S.P. 3rd & Townsend Station)

From Broadway on Kearny to 3rd to S.P. Station. 1.29 miles. (Commuter line)

Start of street car operation. (Peak hour service only) .... *September 15, 1936*
Last day of street car operation .... *September 12, 1941*

(Above) Packed with early morning commuters from SP's 3rd and Townsend station car #822 crosses Market Street entering Kearny on its trek to the financial district. ***Tom Gray photo.*** **(Left) One of the hired hands had a little fun with route designations at the Third Street barn.** ***Tom Gray collection.***

UN-NUMBERED LINES

VISITACION VALLEY
(Mission & Geneva to Six Mile House)

From Mission on Geneva to Walbridge, Schwerin, McDonald, private right-of-way, County Road to Six Mile House at Sunnydale Ave. 2.32 miles.

Start of street car operation .... *October 25, 1909*
Last day of street car operation .... *July 31, 1937*

Ex Williamsport car #735 at Mission and Geneva ready for its run to Six Mile House at Old County Road in 1937. ***Tom Gray photo.***

SOUTH SAN FRANCISCO
(Leipsic Jct. to W.P. Fuller Paint plant)

From Holy Cross to Grand Ave.,across S.P. Tracks to W.P. Fuller Plant. 3.88 miles.

Start of street car operation. .... *December 31, 1903*
Inner terminal changed: Holy Cross to Leipsic Jct. .... *June 18, 1916*
Last day of street car operation .... *December 31, 1938*

At Leipsic Junction connecting point with the #40 line, December 1937. Note car #285 rebuilt as only a one-man car. After line was abandoned car was again changed back to two-man. ***Bert Ward photo.***

Front view of car #285 rebuilt at Elkton shops into a one-man car May 11, 1932 for the South San Francisco line. Note "Lead Works" in destination roller - the W.P. Fuller paint works located at the end of the South San Francisco line.

PARKSIDE
(20th Ave. & Taraval to 35th Ave. & Sloat)

On Taraval from 20th to 33rd Ave., Vicente, 35th Ave. to Sloat Blvd. 1.52 miles.

Start of street car operation .... *Prior 1915*
Last day of street car operation .... *Late 1927*

Several single truck cars such as #603 were converted into one-man cars around 1914. This one was assigned to the Parkside line. When one-man cars were outlawed in San Francisco in 1918, the conductor would stand by the motorman to collect fares. ***Bert Ward collection.***

DIVISADERO EXTENSION
(Divisadero & Sacramento to Divisadero & Jackson)

On Divisadero from Sacramento to Jackson. .18 miles. Shortest line in San Francisco: Three blocks.

Start of street car operation. .... *Prior 1915*
(Ran three uphill blocks connecting with lines 3, 4 & 24)
Last day of street car operation *mid-1930s*

Single truck one-man car #604 assigned to this three-block line. Photo taken at Sacramento and Divisadero. ***Ralph Demoro photo, Harre Demoro collection.***

TENTH & MONTGOMERY
(10th & Bryant to Kearny & Washington)

From Bryant on 10th across Market to Polk, Hayes, Larkin, McAllister, Leavenworth, Post, Montgomery, Washington to Kearny. 2.75 miles.

Start of street car operation .... *Prior 1906*
Outer terminal cut back to Post & Market .... *October 6, 1927*
Last day of street car operation *1932*

Car #803 heads out Post crossing Kearny Street about the year 1915. ***Bert Ward collection.***

BOSWORTH
(Mission & Bosworth to Glen Park)

From Mission on Bosworth to Burnside to Glen Park. 0.73 miles.

Start of street car operation. .... *Prior 1915*
Last day of street car operation .... *By 1928*

Single truck car #614 as a one-man car suffers some damage in a collision and is at the Elkton shops for repairs. ***John Graham collection.***

FIRST & FIFTH
(5th & Market to Battery & California)

From Market on 5th to Brannan, 2nd, Folsom, 1st, across Market to Bush & Sansome, alternating trips to Battery & California. On return, 1st, Folsom, 2nd, Brannan, 3rd, Townsend (SP Station), 4th, Brannan, 5th to Market.

Start of street car operation .... Prior 1915
Last day of street car operation (In part to #42 line) .... By 1930

Single truck one-man car #602 is a type that operated on this line until it was discontinued in the later 1920's. ***Tom Gray collection.***

Year End Sale
Year End Sale

CHAPTER 4

SAN FRANCISCO MUNICIPAL RAILWAY

The seed for the operation of a city owned street car system was sown at the turn of the century. Actually it was in the year 1898, when the citizens of San Francisco ratified a new charter for the City and County of San Francisco that decreed its public utilities shall gradually be acquired and ultimately owned by the City. This was approved by the State Legislature on January 26, 1899, to take effect the following year, January 8, 1900.

With the laying of rail for electric street cars in many directions by the Market Street Railway (United Railroads after 1902), the city fathers were anxious to get started on a city owned railway to be known as The Municipal Railway of San Francisco. The Geary, Park and Ocean Railroad, a cable line extending from Geary and Market, out Geary to 5th Avenue, to Fulton, to 7th Avenue, a total of 3.8 miles was about to see its franchise expire on November 3, 1903. The city officials were ready to take over this cable route and convert it to electric street car operation. However, the people of San Francisco had an aversion to overhead trolley wire. They considered it dangerous. Noting that underground conduit systems were in use in Washington, D.C. and New York City the voters of San Francisco were asked to approve such a system. A December 2, 1902, election killed the plan. The vote was tried again on November 6, 1903. It also went down to defeat.

With gigantic problems of the earthquake and resulting fire on April 18, 1906, the thought of a city owned railway was placed on the back-burner until a year later. In June, 1907, the city budgeted $720,000 for the purchase of the cable system on Geary Street, but this was declared invalid by the courts.

(Left) Thousands came downtown to be on hand for the opening day of the Municipal Railway, December 28, 1912. With Mayor Rolph officiating, the ceremonies took place at Kearny and Geary Streets commencing at 12:30 p.m. ***Muni photo.***

After the disastrous fire in 1906, the city okayed the use of overhead trolley wire on Market Street for the United Railroads, as the private company wanted to replace their five heavily used cable lines on the busy thoroughfare with electric operated street cars. With the danger of the electric system greatly minimized, the city opted for another election on June 24, 1909. It was defeated by a small margin, so the city tried again on December 30, 1909, asking for $2,020,000 in bonds; $1,900,000 for the purchase of the cable line and construction of a street car line on Geary Street and $120,000 for trackage on Market Street from Geary to Sutter to connect with United Railroad tracks to the Ferry Loop. The street car line would extend from Kearny and Market on Geary to 33rd Avenue and on 10th Avenue from Geary to Fulton. The bond issue passed.

With engineering plans completed, preparation began during the summer of 1911. On May 5, 1912, the Geary Street cable railroad ceased operation and reconstruction of the street and roadbed began in earnest.

Forty-three street cars were ordered from W.L. Holman Company, but after delivering 20 cars the company went broke, so the remaining 23 cars were built by the Union Iron Works, San Francisco, which later became Bethlehem Shipyard. The cars were designed by transit consultant Bion J. Arnold, so the cars became known as the "Arnold cars". A car barn was built at Presidio Avenue and Geary Street.

The big day came on December 28, 1912, when street car service was inaugurated and The Municipal Railway of San Francisco became a reality, in fact, the first public owned street railway system in the country. With Mayor "Sunny" Jim Rolph at the controls, and the first ever minted nickel from San Francisco's Mint placed in the five cent fare box, the street cars began rolling. Ten cars had been received from builder, so nine cars were assigned to Geary line to 10th Avenue and to Fulton Street. It became known as the "A" line. The one lone car shuttled on Geary between 10th and 33rd Avenue.

(Above) Looking east on Geary Street 200 feet from the Van Ness Avenue intersection construction crews are busy clearing out old cable yokes and rails. They soon will be laying new rail for Muni's first street car line. Note trolley wire already in place, August 9, 1912. ***Ted Wurn collection.*** **(Below) Patrons board car #26 at Geary and Kearny in the Spring of 1913. Note fashion of the times on lady, left.** ***Bert Ward collection.***

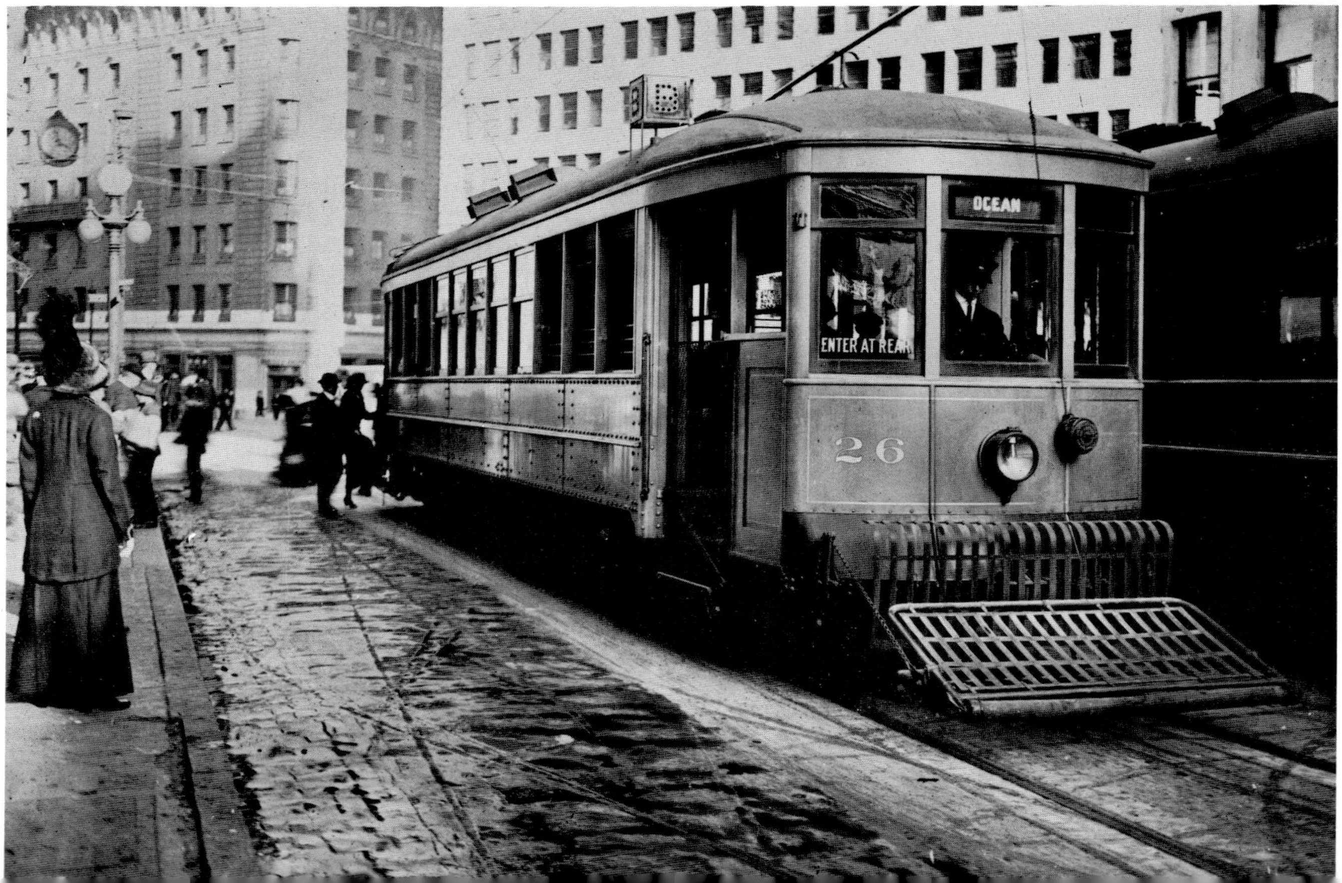

(Left) Presidio & Ferries single truck car #19 at the Ferry Terminal in the year 1913. It went into the 301 series when the Muni took over December 11, 1913, *Tom Gray collection.* (Center) Mayor "Sunny Jim" Rolph hails the beginning of the "H" line with speech from a Muni car at Van Ness and Market on opening day, August 15, 1914. Men wore hats in those days! *Ted Wurm collection.* (Lower) A group of dignitaries pose for a photo at the "H" line opening. Michael O'Shaughnessy, who became city engineer in 1912 and directed the engineering aspects of the new Muni lines being established, is directly below the motorman's window. Mayor Rolph, with derby hat and wearing a flower in his lapel, stands behind young man in light suit, cap and short pants. *Bert Ward collection.*

Car #48 swings from Van Ness to cross Market into 11th Street in the year 1916. Note rear marker lamp, required on cars on the line between 18th and 25th on Potrero; Muni shared trackage with the Ocean Shore Railroad and their rules of the road required the procedure. ***Richard Schlaich collection.***

An agreement was reached between the Municipal Railway and United Railroads as to payment for track use between Sutter Street and the Ferry Loop on Market Street. The Muni constructed its own track outside of United tracks on Market from Geary to Sutter. However, because of franchise restrictions, United had to run a horse car operation from Sutter to the Ferry Loop. No schedule could be maintained with a horse car occupying the tracks, so a city ordinance quickly ended the horse car operation which took place on June 3, 1913. Mayor Rolph was again at the "controls" but this time held the reins of the horse for the final trip. The horse car era in the City by the Bay had officially come to an end.

Meanwhile, construction got underway to extend the Geary line from Geary on 33rd to Balboa, 45th Avenue, Cabrillo to Great Highway at Ocean Beach. This line was opened, June 25, 1913. Again, Mayor "Sunny Jim" Rolph was at the controls of the first car to inaugurate the new extension. This became known as the "B" line. The Muni gave the extension wide publicity that one could ride from the Ferry Terminal to the beaches for a nickel. A loop at Great Highway was installed and ready for service on August 25, 1915.

On February 15, 1911, William H. Taft, President of the United States, signed a document recognizing San Francisco as the city to hold the official Exposition in celebration of the building and completion of the Panama Canal. Dates selected: February 20 to December 4, 1915. The exposition area, 635 acres, would stretch from Van Ness Avenue to the Presidio Army Reservation and from Chestnut Street to San Francisco Bay.

At a meeting of the San Francisco Board of Supervisors, February 5, 1913, Panama-Pacific Exposition President, Charles C. Moore, flatly told the body that there was no adequate street car service to the area and without it, the entire $100 million venture could be doomed to failure. The United Railroads refused to build one inch of additional track account of the stringent city charter amendment, which gave the city the right to purchase any line or lines provided by future franchise grants. The city engineers went to work to come up with plans for new city owned street car lines. A $3.5 million bond issues passed on August 26, 1913. Funds became available on January 1, 1914.

After that date there was feverish activity in building new lines as submitted by the City's Engineering Department. The bond issue would include street car routes that would follow practically the same lines in later years; C, D, E, F, J, and H. The "E" route would result from the take over of the Presidio and Ferries Railroad, which company's franchise was about to expire. It ran from the Presidio to the Ferry, North Terminal. This company had 29 single truck street cars in their fleet of 1890 vintage that had been purchased from the United Railroads after the earthquake and fire in 1906 when they changed over from a cable car system. The transfer took place on December 11, 1913. Purchase price $312,323, which payment was made in January, 1914. Because of the rickety old track it had to be almost completely replaced. The job was completed on February 10, 1915.

With the clock moving toward the Exposition opening date, track construction on Van Ness Avenue and Chestnut Street was intense, with Mahoney Brothers receiving the contract. Work commenced on April 6, 1914 with completion on August 4, 1914, along with the installation of poles and overhead trolley wire. The street car service on Van Ness known as the "H" line began service on August 15, 1914. The south of Market, Eleventh Street and Potrero construction went to Eaton and Smith. This section also to be used by the "H' line was ready for service on September 17, 1914. Between 18th and 25th on Potrero a joint use agreement was established with the Ocean Shore Railroad owners of this section of track. Trackage on Scott, Greenwich and Steiner was also completed in September. The Fort Mason Loop, which had been okayed by the Military, was placed in operation in October, 1914, and would be the terminus for the "H" line.

For the Stockton Street "F" line, Bion Arnold, Transit consultant, had recommended the construction of a tunnel beneath the Nob Hill area between Bush and Sacramento Streets. This caused numerous arguments pro and con, so it was not until August 26, 1912, that the project was approved. Contract for the tunnel construction went to Jacobsen-Bade Company, April 11, 1913. For the track installation on Stockton Street, Columbus and North Point went to Rolandi Company. The contract also included the placing of the Fort Mason Loop tracks.

The 911-foot concrete Stockton Street tunnel was completed in December, 1914. It was cause for a big celebration on December 28, 1914, with Chinatown, where the line traverses for several blocks, going all out with a brilliant pagentry of golden dragons and upbeat music. The following day was inaugural day for the "F" street car line. Once again "Sunny" Jim was at the controls of the lead car as it moved slowly amid a crush of citizens who had come to view the festivities. Most of the Arnold cars 1-43, were assigned to this new line.

Construction scene of the south end of the Stockton Street tunnel, July 17, 1914. Rails and overhead wire were still to come when this photo was taken. Inauguration day took place, December 24, 1914. ***Ted Wurm collection.***

For service over the several new lines, the Muni ordered 125 new street cars of the California type from the Jewett Car Company, to be numbered 44 thorough 168. The cars, known as the "B" type, began arriving in July, 1914, in time for the start of the "D" and "H" lines the following month and also to take over the runs of the "B" line, where the Arnold cars were being shifted to the "F" line.

Then came the opening day of the Panama-Pacific Exposition, February 20, 1915. It was a gala day and the Muni was ready. Lines "A", "B", and "C" transferred Fair patrons at either Van Ness to the "D" or "H" line or at Stockton Street to the "F" line. For the first three days of the Exposition the "B" line had cars that ran direct to the Exposition grounds and for that short time was known as the "I" line. Also established for the Ex-

Known as Type "B", 125 of these cars were built by Jewett Car Company in 1913. Note open end sections, which were enclosed in the 1920s. ***Bert Ward collection.***

(Above) In the first two weeks of the 1915 Panama-Pacific Exposition there were over one million visitors. The Muni with its 197 street cars at the time was stretched to capacity to handle the crowds. Photo shows Muni car at one of the four entrances to the popular Fair. *Ted Wurm collection.* (Left) Car #25 poses at the ''C'' line's outer terminus at 33rd and California. *Guido collection.* (Lower) Masonic Avenue stub line ran three blocks from Geary to Turk in order to handle crowds for Ewing Field (Football and baseball). The stub was used only on game days. Car #181 poses on this section of track, November 15, 1923. *Ted Wurm collection.*

On August 4, 1917, thousands flocked to Mission Dolores Park to see the opening of the "J" line, which was on grade and private right-of-way through a section of the park between 18th and 20th Streets. ***Tom Gray collection.***

position was the "G" line from downtown Stockton and Market via Union Street to the Presidio, and the "J" line (not to be confused with the later "J" line) from the Ferries north terminal via Columbus to the Fort Mason Loop. A total of 197 street cars were available for the operation, numbered 1-168 and 301-329.

Attendance on opening day of the Exposition numbered 246,738. Total for the first 14 days came to 1,036,349. To handle the crowds entering the Exposition there were four entrances; Van Ness, Fillmore, Scott and Baker, the latter three on Chestnut Street. The Muni did a beautiful job, so much so, that the Board of Supervisors passed a resolution commending the officials and employees for a job well done.

The bond issue of 1913 provided for the construction of a car barn and service facility at 17th and Potrero. This was completed in 1914 in time for the operation of the "H" line cars.

The bond issue also included the building of the "C' line. This route would take off Geary on to 2nd Avenue thence to Cornwall into California Street at 6th Avenue and continue to 33rd Avenue. The section between 6th and 33rd on California included the United Railroads car line #1 rails on this portion, however, as the franchise expired on September 5, 1914, the city took it over. United Railroads moved their #1 line over one block to Clement Street. Because of the slowness in selling the bonds, the start of building the "C" line was stalled until December 14, 1914. After that time rapid progress took place. The section that belonged to United Railroads was entirely rebuilt. The "C" line was opened to 13th Avenue the day before the opening of the Fair, February 19, 1915 and to 33rd Avenue on March 28, 1915.

At this point in history, it should be mentioned that a quarter mile of track was built on Masonic Avenue off Geary to serve the new Ewing Field ballpark. It was ready for service, May 16, 1914.

Next in the expansion of the Muni was the building of the present "J" line. While the original intent of the city fathers was to build the line from monies obtained from a proposed assessment district, the complaints were loud and clear. The funds to build the line from Church and Market on Church to 30th, with a private right-of-way along the Mission Dolores Park, had to come from the issuance of bonds. While the actual okay to start the construction took place December, 1914, legal snarls developed with United Railroads regarding the crossing of their tracks at 24th, 20th, 16th and Market at Church. In addition, whether it should be a joint operation with United Railroads on Church between Market and 16th with their #22 line and on Market between Church and Van Ness with the #8 line. In June, 1915, the section between 16th and 30th was ready to start, but the legal battles continued at other crossings whether to travel over or parallel the United's tracks for two blocks on Church and six blocks on Market. On June 2, 1916, the city passed an ordinance for the construction of parallel tracks on Church and on Market from Church all the way to Geary to hook up with parallel track already in place. There were more starts and stops. However, August 11, 1917, saw the official opening of the "J" line. Mayor Rolph was again on hand and piloted the first car from Mission Dolores Park to 30th and thence back to Market and to the Ferry Loop via Van Ness and Geary. The "J" line was now in service from 30th and Church to Van Ness and Market. It was extended to Pine and Van Ness, August 29, 1917. The Van Ness operation was ended when the parallel tracks on Market were in place and the cars rolled right down Market to the Ferry Loop, June 1, 1918.

(Above) Geary and Market, February 14, 1917. Note Muni tracks on Market, west beyond Geary, have yet to be installed. ***Ted Wurm collection.*** **(Below) Busy downtown scene at 4th and Market in the early 1920's.** ***Tom Gray collection.***

(Upper left) Car #113 with Mayor "Sunny Jin" Rolph at the controls emerges from the west portal of the Twin Peaks tunnel on inauguration day, February 3, 1918, for Muni's new "K" line. ***Tom Gray collection.*** **(Upper Right) Hard to believe West Portal in 1919. Today, it is a street with business establishments on both sides, and homes on every lot in the hilly terrain.** ***Bert Ward collection.*** **(Above) Opening ceremonies, February 3, 1918, were held at St. Francis circle and West Portal, terminus of the newly established "K" line at the time. From the massive wave of "hats" it looks as if only men attended the festivities.** ***Ted Wurm collection.***

To properly serve the area west of Twin Peaks and develop the Ingleside district and the Sunset area sand dunes into residential property, a railway tunnel under Twin Peaks would give direct and fast service. To give the push that was needed the Twin Peak Tunnel Improvement Club was formed. An assessment district was established which would include approximately 5,000 acres. The tunnel proposed would be 12,000 feet in length, 25 feet wide and 15 feet above the rails. With approval of the assessment district, the contract for the drilling of the bore went to Robert C. Storrie & Company, on November 12, 1914 for a bid of $3,372,000. The work commenced on both ends; 17th, Castro and Market Streets and West Portal on November 30, 1914. The east end was constructed so as to allow for a subway connection under Market Street in future years, which did not come to fruition until 60 years later. The final cost of the tunnel came to $4,250,000.

While the tunnel was under construction United Railroads was vying for position. They had their #12 Ingleside-Sloat Boulevard line in place to the beach and their Parkside line on Taraval from 20th to 35th Avenue and Sloat. A connection with their #8 Market line through the tunnel would give their patrons fast service from a developing residential area to downtown. United figured Muni had to have tracks to the East Portal while United already had theirs in place with the #8 line to Castro and 17th. This caused some stormy sessions. All United proposals were rejected with a final decision by San Francisco to build two outer tracks on Market from Church to the East Portal, so Muni would have direct access to the tunnel.

The Twin Peaks tunnel was opened with gala ceremonies on July 14, 1917. Rails were then quickly laid on Market for the three blocks between Castro and Church. The grand opening took place, February 3, 1918. Once again Mayor Rolph was at the controls, as he guided the official street car #113 on the first trip. With the Municipal Band playing all the popular tunes of the day, a large crowd came out for the festivities and cheered #113 as it moved into the tunnel. All in all a grand day in the expansion of the Muni.

(Above) A bird's eye view of the Ferry Loop and its three tracks. Note pedestrian bridge built in the early 1920s, also "E" car at North Ferry street car terminal. Photo taken March 28, 1930. *Ted Wurm collection.* (Below) Scene at Geary, Kearny and Market in the early 1920s. Note San Francisco landmark, Lotta's Fountain in center, given to the city by famed vaudville entertainer and singer, Lotta Crabtree in 1875. It survived the 1906 quake, although the top portion was raised eight feet in 1916 to new level of street light standards. The fountain is still in existence today, unlike street car line "A" to the right and #32 lower left, which were phased out in 1932. *Tom Gray collection.*

Car #43 trundles along the right-of-way near 19th Avenue and Eucalyptus Street in 1933. Today, homes completely surround the right-of-way. *Bert Ward collection.*

The outer tracks had not been laid on Market Street from Van Ness to Geary, so the cars turned on Van Ness and established the end of the line at Pine Street. The Market Street Van Ness-Geary section was completed on June 1, 1918, and cars then ran direct on Market to the Ferry Loop.

The immediate effect of through Market Street service was 40 more cars per hour at the Ferry Loop, causing a jam of cars at peak hours. The State Harbor Commission gave permission to construct a 3rd loop, August 22, 1918. When completed the number of cars using the Ferry loops were 290 cars per hour; 110 on the inner circle, 80 on the middle and 100 on the outer track. To ease the congestion a pedestrian footbridge from the 2nd floor of the Ferry Building across the Embarcadero was built in 1920. With four tracks on Market Street the famous thoroughfare became known as the "Roar of the Four" with its many street cars trundling back and forth. A total of 21 lines fed into the street; 12 Market Street Railway and 9 Municipal Railway.

The next step on the outer end of the Twin Peaks tunnel was to establish the "L" line. The okay by the Board of Supervisors came on September 25, 1917 to build a double track from West Portal to Ulloa, 15th Avenue, Taraval, to 20th to connect with United Railroad's Parkside line. Negotiations with United allowed the Muni to operate on a joint track basis between 20th and 33rd on Taraval was okayed on November 25, 1918. The track was rebuilt with service commencing, April 12, 1919.

Also negotiated with United Railroads was the use of trackage from Sloat Boulevard at St. Francis Circle to Ocean Avenue to Harold and later to Brighton. With connections completed the new "K" line began operations to Ocean and Harold, February 21, 1919. The extension to Ocean and Brighton and thence to Grafton was in service, May 18, 1919.

Another new line into a sparse area, known as the "M" line, commenced operation on October 6, 1925. From St. Francis Circle the new tracks went on a private right-of-way to and including the center of 19th Avenue, thence Randolph, Orizaba, Broad to Plymouth Streets.

Like all transportation systems, World War I brought on a tremendous increase in patronage. While the Muni did not directly serve shipyards and industrial areas the railway brought thousands of workers to United Railroad connections.

With World War I in high gear, United Railroad carmen walked off their cars, August 12, 1917, in demand for wage parity with Muni platform men. The United States War Shipping Board concerned over a ship building slow down appealed for emergency service. Out of it came an agreement for Muni to operate steam trains supplied by the Ocean Shore Railroad from the shipyards over Southern Pacific tracks to the Ocean Shore along Army Street to their shops at Army and Potrero. Half the trains proceeded over Ocean Shore to their Daly City station by steam train and the other half along Potrero, Mariposa, 12th Street to the Ocean Shore station at 12th and Mission by electric motors. Muni railway conductors were assigned to these trains

(Above) Geary Barn located at Presidio and Geary in its hey-day of street cars, April 12, 1923. Eleven street cars can be seen. The main office of the Muni still exists in this location (1990) but the barn services only trolley coaches on the lower level. *Red Wurm collection.* (Lower) Again, "Sunny Jim" Rolph is at the controls of the first car for the new "N" line as it emerges from Sunset tunnel, October 21, 1918. Crowds atop the tunnel cheer as the car comes into view. *Tom Gray collection.*

with a fare of five cents including transfers to connecting Muni street car lines. On September 15, 1917, the shipyard workers went on strike, which resulted in the discontinuance of the shipyard trains. However, public pressure kept the trains going between Army Street shop area to Daly City, 5:30 a.m. to 11:00 p.m. connecting with the Muni ''H'' line at Army Street. On September 30th, the shipyard workers went back to work and the steam trains resumed to the shipyards. The United Railroad strike came to an end on November 24, 1917, so Muni's short-lived period of operating steam trains came to an end.

The last major extension of the city owned railway was slated for south of Golden Gate Park and north of Taraval Street. Soon after the Panama-Pacific Exposition in 1915, the city engineers came up with a plan to extend the ''A'' line from Fulton and 10th Avenue across Golden Gate Park to Judah and thence westward to the beach. This was promptly nixed by the mayor, who firmly stated that no new rail lines would be placed in the park at any location. (United #7 line near the beach was already in place). Plans for a new street car line in the area lay dormant until 1921, when a tunnel was proposed under Buena Vista Park ridge. In anticipation of this line, twenty street cars known as the K type, were ordered from Bethlehem Shipbuilding Corp., San Francisco. They were delivered between July and November, 1923 and numbered 169-188. There was much pro and con, but finally on June 10, 1926, steam shovels began digging a tunnel from Doboce and Scott on the east side, and Cole and Carl on the west for a total of 4,232 feet. Youdall Construction did the work for $1,247,592 with the job completed on August 17, 1927, and concrete lining in place two months later. The tunnel became known as the Sunset tunnel.

(Below) Car #50 was destroyed by fire at the Geary and Presidio car barn paint shop, November 27, 1934. The car was scrapped and never replaced. Photo shows how it looked before scrapping. December 4, 1934. ***Muni photo.***

Market Street at 3rd with "K" car in foreground and Palace Hotel at right March 15, 1927. *Ted Wurm collection.*

21
CLEMENT

(Above) Scene at the North Ferry Terminal opening day of the Golden Gate International Exposition, February 18, 1939. Every third "F" car was routed to this terminal during weekends and holidays. *Bert Ward photo.* (Center) With the Exposition held at Treasure Island in San Francisco Bay in 1939-40, the Muni decided to change decor of their cars from dull gray to deep blue and orangey yellow. First car with the new paint scheme was #154 as shown at end of the "L" line in 1939. *Muni photo.* (Lower) All yellow front was changed to blue below window sash, as shown by car #80 in June 1942. Photo taken at 48th and Taraval. 5 cent fare still in effect! *Will Whittaker photo.*

A "B" car from Geary Street tries to get into the line up on Market heading either for the Ferry Building or the East Bay Terminal during the World War II year of 1942. ***Tom Gray collection.***

While taxpayer suits stalled the work from time to time, the rails were finally in place to Ocean Beach with the inaugural run set for October 21, 1928. Once again "Sunny" Jim Rolph was at the controls of the lead street car. (He was Mayor of San Francisco for 19 years; June 8, 1912 to January 7, 1931 during all of the construction days of the Muni). It was another day of festivity for the city by the Golden Gate with two bands; Municipal and Railway outdoing themselves whipping up the popular tunes as the official car ambled along the new line with its gaily decorated flags and bunting. It concluded with a huge carnival at Ninth Avenue and Irving Street that evening.

The new line was designated as the "N" line. It was popular from the start as had been predicted. As all lines were showing increased patronage, the Muni ordered 25 more street cars known as the "L" type. The successful bidder was the St. Louis Car Company. Numbered 189-213, the first 15 arrived on June 15, 1927 with the remaining ten by March 15, 1928. They would be the last of this type to be purchased.

With Muni having expanded to its desired construction goals, the city fathers noted that Market Street Railway franchises were about to expire and had thoughts to take over the private railway. It came up for a vote in November, 1928, but this time the voters said "no". They thought it better to have competition and also give the Market Street Railway a new lease on life by granting the private railroad new franchises for all its lines for a period of 25 years. The Market Street Railway, so enthused with the voter's decision built a new line #31 on Turk and Balboa Street to 30th Avenue, which spelled the doom of Muni's "A" line. It was discontinued December 5, 1932.

With a rearrangement of "D", "E" and "H" lines, Muni started a new line, known as the "O" line from Market and Van Ness to the Presidio, June 1, 1932. Intense opposition immediately developed with the result the "O" line was shortlived, being discontinued a month later, July 15.

During the latter months of 1938, there was feverish activity on man-made Treasure Island in San Francisco Bay to complete the various buildings for the opening of the Golden Gate International Exposition set for February 18, 1939. At the same time, the city fathers gazing out of their windows at City Hall, could not help but notice the Market Street Railway cars on the #5 McAllister line with their immaculate new paint scheme of forest green, white streamline flourish on the sides, and a bright yellow roof. The Muni's drab gray with maroon window sash and tile red roof needed some brightening, so the California colors of blue and gold were adopted. The first street car in the new decor to hit the streets was #154 in the summer of 1939. The sides were blue and the window sash and front ends were an orangey yellow to resemble gold. The gold was also applied on the roof over the platforms with a rusty gray. Btween the roof and body was a cardinal red stripe. When the "magic carpet" cars arrived in October, 1939, a lighter yellow was substituted for the gold color. The roof was changed to all yellow color. During 1940-1945 practically all the Muni cars were thusly painted, except the "dinkies" 351-371, which remained gray.

(Above) Bird's eye view of the three tracks serving the Bay Bridge Transit Terminal, more commonly known as the East Bay Terminal. Cars turned off Market at First, thence across Mission into terminal and loop into Fremont back to Market. Photo taken August 28, 1947. *Muni photo.* (Below) The new "magic carpet" car #1001 on display at the Ferry Building, November 1939. They were the first with the streamline PCC look in San Francisco. *Bert Ward photo.*

(Above) Car #1 poses for 30th birthday occasion at the Geary barn, December 28, 1942. Some interesting statistics, but for #1 the retirement never came. Today (1990) it is in Festival street car service. Note Christmas greeting in window from Mayor Rossi! *Muni collection.* (Below) There have been very few photos of the east end of the Twin Peaks tunnel. Here is one, with "magic carpet" car #1002 in the foreground at 17th and Castro, June 7, 1942. *Arthur Lloyd photo.*

(Above) Many of the old Market Street cars were worn out. #136, for some reason jumped the track at Market near Powell, causing a huge back up on July 26, 1947, *Smallwood photo, Ted Wurm collection.* (Left) In early 1946 car #211 came out with all yellow front as shown in this photo as car ambles along 33rd Avenue near Balboa. *Will Whittaker photo.*

A narrow vertical stripe design was given car #94, the only car to receive this type of format. Photo taken 1946 at terminus of the "N" line at Judah and La Playa. *Bert Ward photo.*

In 1946, Car #56 came out with a "V" on its front; presumably indicating "V" for victory. It was the only Muni car to get this design. Photo taken on Market Street as the car glides by the Emporium on its outward trek on the "L" line. *Tom Gray collection.*

(Above) In 1946 the blue "V" on yellow fronts made their debut on 36 former Market Street cars. Cars with asterisk (*) had the small "V", those underlined were also given complete yellow and blue sides, such as car #170 above, the only Jewett to receive the complete blue and yellow paint decor with the "V" front. Photo taken at 12th and Lincoln Way, May 19, 1946. "V" cars were: 132, 136, 150, 156, 166, 170, 175, 203, 231, 243, 256, 264, 267*, 275, 284, 296, 300, 802, 803, 823, 825, 837, 845, 864, 867, 913 927, 948*, 964, 976, 978, 979, 1232, 1234, 1716, and 1722. (Philip Hoffman data) ***Art Lloyd photo.*** **(Below) When Muni took over the Market Street Railway, September 29, 1944, it did not include the patented white front design, so Muni went about changing the front appearance. Some 146 cars were painted with blue and yellow fronts, 12 a short-lived yellow, 36 with "V" fronts (7 of these received the blue and yellow sides) and 14, as this photo shows, complete blue and yellow front and sides; 147, 1227, 1229, 1230, 1232-1236, 1238, 1241, 1243, 1244, and 887, the latter with "Training Car-No Passengers" lettered on its sides. Car #1244 on San Mateo Drive, San Mateo, October 11, 1945.** ***Art Lloyd photo.***

A scene that would be repeated many times in the late 1940s, the demise of street car lines. On July 2, 1949, it was goodbye to Sutter Street lines, 1, 2 and 3. Actually this was a special last trip taken two days later for invited guests. It was sad to see, at the right, what took the place of the street cars. *Muni photo.*

When the Bay Bridge terminal between First and Fremont on Mission opened on January 15, 1939, half of the cars serving the Ferry Loop on Market were rerouted to the new terminal (See Routes section for details).

Also, in 1939, the ''M'' line was discontinued on August 6 because of poor patronage, however, the rails were kept in place. On December 17, 1944, the street car line was re-established.

During the early 1930's the Electric Railway **P**resident's **C**onference **C**ommittee, which had been studying to design a modern street car produced plans that would be known as the PCC car. The first car in service in the U.S.A. took place in Brooklyn, New York, on October 1, 1936. It was the beginning of a production of almost 5,000 cars of this type to be built for cities in the U.S.A. and Canada. The Muni ordered five of the design, but they were not the true PCC car, as the Muni did not wish to pay for some of the patents involved. The five cars, numbered 1001-1005, known as the ''magic carpet'' cars were delivered, October 31, 1939.

With the start of World War II, December 7, 1941 and gasoline rationing on December 1, 1942, Muni, like all transportation systems in the country, became a beehive of activity. Many employees were called or volunteered for various branches of the Armed Services. Appeals went out for older citizens and women to become platform personnel or do maintenance work. The appeal ads appeared on many of the street cars sides in attractive eye-catching decor.

While the electorate of San Francisco had defeated five bond issues for the acquisition of the Market Street Railway (November 1, 1925; September 27, 1938; November 8, 1939; November 3, 1942; April 20, 1943), the voters became well aware of the plight of the private railway; it was in a state of collapse. With this in mind they approved the purchase of the Market Street Railway for a sum of $7.5 million on May 16, 1944. The takeover, which included 440 street cars (74 unoperable) and 217.034 miles of single track of which 28.06 was in San Mateo County, took place at 5:00 a.m., September 29, 1944. The purchase involved 25 street car lines.

To reveal how bad it was, E.G. Cahill, Manager of San Francisco's Public Utilities, stated ''The entire former Market Street Railway will have to be scrapped immediately after the war, in fact, if the war lasts too long, it will scrap itself. It is obvious that the equipment, every piece, which must be dragged off to the barns for repairs 15 times in five months, is in the last stages of decrepitude. It will be a miracle if this rambling wreck of a railway can be held together for the duration, regardless of the amount of money we spend on it.''

With the purchase some of the street cars had identical numbers, so to eliminate any confusion, the Market cars in the 100 series that were operable were given 400 numbers and those in the 200 class, 600 numbers.

In early 1946, car #211 appeared with an all yellow front. Also car #56, but with a blue ''V'' presumably indicating ''V'' for victory, a much heralded slogan at the time. #94 came out with a smaller ''V'' on its yellow front.

As to the ex Market Street Railway cars, 36 received the yellow front with the blue ''V'', a few had the complete paint job, sides and fronts in the blue and yellow theme. All other operable ex Market cars were given yellow fronts and even a silver color, so as to eliminate the white front, as Muni did not purchase the old Market Street Railway patent rights.

Appearing on the streets in June 1946, came another paint decor: cream and green. Five Muni cars were painted thus: 47, 53, 111, 153 and 167. The public favored the bright new colors, so they were adopted. Car #153 at Mission Ferry terminal rerouted account parade on Market Street. *Tom Gray photo.*

Four ex Market Street cars received the cream and green treatment in 1946, #601 (ex #201) as shown at Market and Castro in 1948, and #665, 958 and 1225. *Tom Gray collection.*

As soon as the war was over and things began settling down, the carnage of the Market Street Railway cars began. It was greatly helped by a five-point bond issue, November 4, 1947, totalling $50,150,000, which called for complete modernization (of the times); disposal of all ex Market cars plus the outmoded car barns substituting buses and trolley coaches. In just five short years the entire Market Street Railway street cars numbering 440 were gone along with most of the lines they ran on. A tabulation shows the last day of street car operation on the 25 lines:

January 20, 1945	Line 35
February 3, 1945	Line 26
September 29, 1945	Line 19
December 21, 1945	Line 17
October 7, 1946	Line 15
September 27, 1947	Line 20
June 6, 1948	Lines 5, 21
July 3, 1948	Line(s) 6,7
July 31, 1948	Line(s) 4,22,25
August 13, 1948	Line 27
October 31, 1948	Line 12
January 15, 1949	Line(s) 9,11,14,40,41
July 2, 1949	1,2,3,8,31

As to the above, four Market Street Railway lines became part of the Muni system: #26 south of Army Street to the "H" line; #20, south of Market on Fourth to the S.P. Station to the "F" line; #41 S.P. Station to 2nd and Market to the "F" line; #12 St. Francis Circle on Junipero Serra to Ocean to Brighton and from Brighton on Ocean to Onondaga and Mission to the "K" line.

With the Ferry boats on San Francisco Bay breathing their last on July 20, 1958, trolley coaches and buses took over what was left of lower Market Street patronage. The street cars terminated their many years of serving the Ferry Loop on March 27, 1949. Henceforth all street cars would be routed to the Bay Bridge-East Bay Terminal.

While the Market tracks were being rebuilt from four to two tracks, the Muni established their only numbered street car line, #32. This route was necessary as all lines feeding into Market Street ended at Market and passengers would transfer to the #32 line to continue to their destination. The line started on March 14, 1948 and ended June 6, 1948. Only ex Market cars were used for the short-lived operation.

In 1946, Muni car #47 came out with a new color style. The sides were green with a cream decorative stripe and window sash, ends and roof also in cream. The public was asked to choose whether they wanted this new decor or retain the blue and yellow. The green and cream won out, so car #53, 111, 153, and 167 along with ex Market cars 601, 665, 958 and 1225 received the new green and cream livery. At this point the Muni decided to add an artistic touch, that of cream wings on the sides at both ends. All of the Muni cars received this treatment by 1949, which also included over 50 of the operable ex Market Street cars. Magic Carpet #1001 was the first to come out with the new green and cream design in October, 1946.

During the late 1940's the Muni added two safety features to some of their cars. All of the 44-49, 51-213

With cream and green in public favor, the Muni decided to go one step further and add cream wings to each end. "Magic Carpet" car #1001 was the first out of the paint shop with the "New look", October, 1946. Photo taken at St. Francis Circle, November 2, 1946. *Bert Ward photo.*

All Muni cars, except the 351-371 "dinkey" class received the green and cream with wing design. Photo shows "K" car #59 at Mission Ferry terminal rerouted because of parade on Market Street in 1949. *Tom Gray collection.*

By the late 1940s all Muni cars 44-49, 51-213 had their eclipse fenders removed and replaced with safety bars and the group 150-213 received entrance folding doors, as shown on car #159 as it rolls along the "L" line on Ulloa Street in 1949. *Tom Gray collection.*

Over 50 ex Market Street cars received the Muni cream, green and wing design. #1553 was the only one of the six left of this type car to receive the treatment. Car poses for photo on Golden Gate Park #7 right-of-way in 1948. *Guido collection.*

group (#50 had been destroyed in a paint shop fire in 1934) had their eclipse fenders removed and safety bars installed, in the late 1940's. The safety bars had been purchased from the East Bay Transit System, Oakland, who discontinued their street cars in favor of buses in 1948. The cost was $1.00 per bar. The 150-213 group also received folding entrance doors, which had been salvaged from scrapped Market Street cars. None of the Arnold car 1-43 were included in this program.

The surge to trolley coaches and buses gained momentum; in fact, transit studies made by DeLeuw Cather & Company, Col. Sydney Bingham and Col. Marmion D. Mills recommended keeping only the Muni tunnel lines and the Geary (B) and Stockton (F) surface lines. The "E" Union Street line ended on June 8, 1947; the "D" Geary-Van Ness-Presidio and the "H" Potrero on March 15, 1950; and even the "F" Stockton line fell victim to the demise of the street car with the last operation, January 19, 1951. The "B" and "C" lines that had been planned for partial subway went by the boards too, with the last operation on December 29, 1956.

Sweeping the country around this period was a consortium of bus, tire and gasoline interests known as the National City Lines. It was their purpose to buy up all city street car lines throughout the nation and replace them with buses. When this feat had been accomplished they would push for Municipal ownership along with contracts for gas and maintenance supplies produced by this consortium. San Francisco with its electrical power coming from their own power houses in the Sierra, gave the National City Line outfit the cold shoulder. The tunnel lines K-L-M and N and the non-tunnel "J" survived to stay street car operated. How the "J" line escaped the carnage of the street car was the dogged determination of the politicians living in the area to retain the line. Fortunately they won out.

To augment the remaining street car lines, the Muni purchased ten double end, two-man operation PCC cars from the St. Louis Car Company in 1948. They were given numbers 1006-1015 and designated type "D" and nick-named "Torpedoes". They arrived with the "wings" color format on the sides of each end.

Another order for the same type, but with a single end and center entrance for two-man car operation, was concluded in 1951. Delivery took place in the winter of 1951-52 with the "wings" design only on the front end. They were numbered 1016-1040. These cars would be the last PCC cars built in the U.S.A., therefore #1040 would have the distinction of being the last PCC car built. It has been retained by Muni (1990) as a festival car.

In 1954, the voters of San Francisco approved one-man operation for the street cars. With that, the 1001-1040 streamline cars were converted to one-man operation. Double-enders 1001-1005 had their doors removed from the left side along with several of the 1006-1015 group. Others had their "blind" doors sealed with side bench seats installed where the door wells had been located. As they came out of the paint shops, the cars sported the "wings" only on the entrance side. The first of the one-man streamline cars appeared on the "K" and "L" lines on September 12, 1954, and on the "N" line on January 16, 1955. The Arnold cars 1-43, and the Iron Monsters 44-49, 51-213 remained as two-man cars.

"My wheels are flat; My body sags; My upholstery is in rags. Please vote yes on 1 thru 7; so I can go to Street Car Heaven." So read the inscription on Sand Car #0601 when the Muni was looking to voters for funds to "modernize" their transit vehicles in 1947. #0601 had the last laugh, it did not go to street car heaven, but heaven right here on earth. It was restored to its former 1895 elegance as Hayes O'Farrell #578, by Elkton shops in 1956. Today (1990) it is used for historical occasions in San Francisco as a working old-time trolley. ***Will Whittaker collection.***

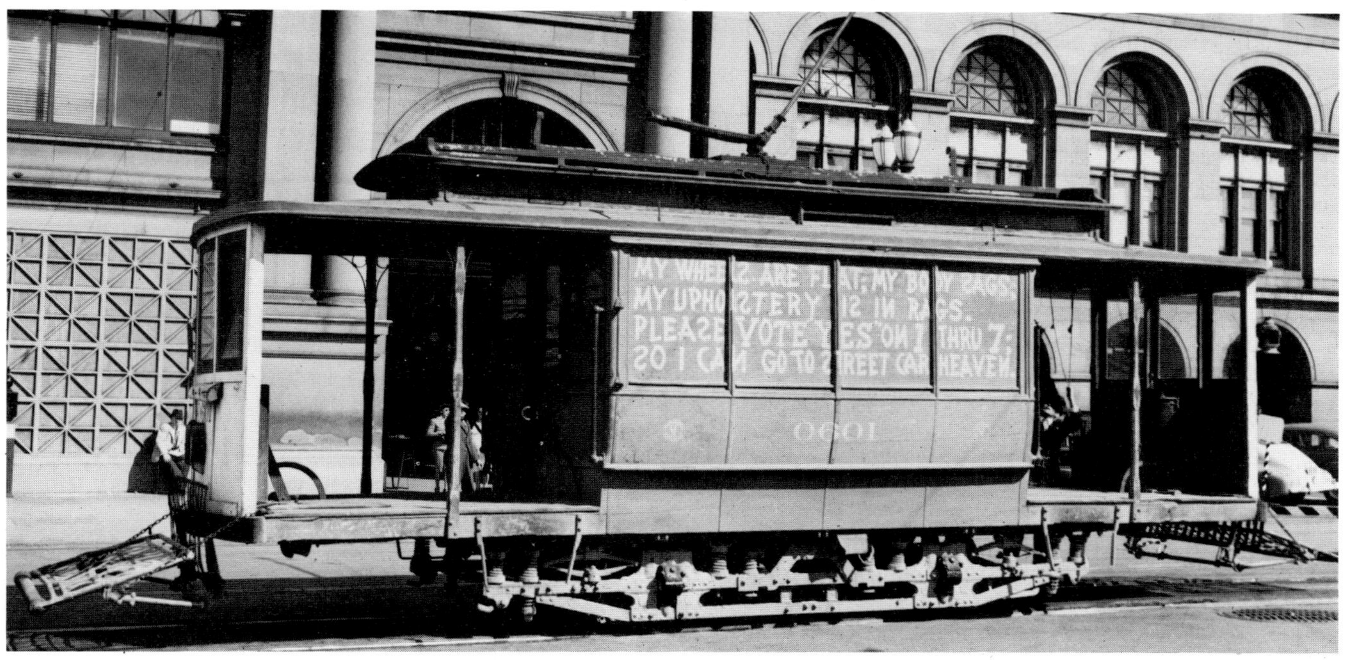

The PCC type ''D'' #1006-1015 nicknamed ''torpedoes'' arrive in 1948 in the new green, cream and wing design as shown by #1008 at the East Bay Terminal that same year. Note ''WP'' (Western Pacific) sign in background, now gone as is the name of the railroad—now Union Pacific. ***Guido collection.***

When the voters of San Francisco okayed the one-man cars the rear doors were removed or sealed and the rear wings eliminated as shown by car #1015 at the East Bay Terminal. ***Guido collection.***

When the PCC group 1016-1040 arrived in 1951-52, the Muni was still two-man operated, passengers boarding at the center entrance. Note wing design only at front. Photo taken at 47th and Wawona, terminus of the ''L'' line in 1953. ***Guido collection.***

Car #1143 on ''K'' line Phelan Loop. Because of large side ads the cream wings were removed from about 60% of the cars. ***Will Whittaker photo.***

In 1963 still another paint scheme appeared on car #1144, with more cream than green design. It was not adopted. ***Will Whittaker photo.***

A golden opportunity presented itself in 1957, when through a lease-purchase agreement, the Muni obtained 66 PCC cars from the St. Louis Public Service, Inc., who was discontinuing some street car lines. The cars arrived with the new green and cream format, numbered 1101-1166. They were built by the St. Louis Car Company in 1946. The Muni purchased them outright in 1964.

As the 1100's took over the remaining five street car routes with the 1001-1040 already in service, the Arnold cars and the Iron Monsters started to disappear. The demise of these cars began in 1951 with the last in service, #181 on the "L" line, May 9, 1954. Several were saved for museum purposes and one for a repair car (see roster section).

The 1001-1005 cars were retired in 1959. Car #1003 went to the Western Railway museum at Rio Vista, California.

Four more PCC cars were obtained from the St. Louis Public Service, Inc., all built by the St. Louis Car Company. Leased in 1962 and purchased in 1964, they became 1167-1170.

In 1963, still another experimental paint scheme appeared on car #1144. All cream with two green borders on the sides. This, however, was not adopted. In the same year, because of ad signs covering most of the "wings", the Muni eliminated the "wings" on about 60% of the cars when they came into the paint shops. Cream and green bands became the new look.

Due to subway construction under Market Street, a round about detour via Duboce off Market to Church, 17th and then to Twin Peaks tunnel was necessary. This required additional street cars. A number of spare PCC cars were available in Toronto, Canada, so eleven were purchased in 1974 and given numbers 1180-1190. They retained their Canadian maroon and buff color. The cars were built for the Kansas City Public Service by the St. Louis Car Company in 1946 (#1190 in 1947). In 1957 they were sold to the Toronto Transportation Commission. All went into service except #1184 (which almost did) and #1185. They had a short life on the Muni. Most operators did not like the cars because of interlock door problems. All were scrapped in 1979, except #1183 and #1190, which were donated to museums-see Roster section.

In the year 1962, the voters of San Francisco, Alameda and Contra Costa Counties approved a Bay Area Rapid Transit District (BART), which would build three lines in the East Bay from Fremont, Concord and Richmond into Oakland and thence under San Francisco Bay and under Market Street to a final point in Daly City. It would also construct a subway for Muni above the BART system along Market Street to Twin Peaks tunnel for the K-L-M lines and an off shoot at Duboce to come to the surface just before the intersection of Church and Duboce for the "J" and "N" lines. BART also received the contract to redo the Twin Peaks tunnel and the station facility at West Portal. There were numerous delays with law suits and strikes, but finally the work started for the Market Street subways in June, 1967.

(Above) In 1974 Muni purchased eleven PCCs from Toronto, Canada. #1180 shown at Duboce and Market, June 1974. (Right above and lower) #1184 almost made it in service, but #1185 never came close. Idle in yard across street from Geneva barn in 1977. ***Stindt photos.***

(Above) For passenger entertainment car #1014 and one other had movie projectors installed. Mid-1970s exact date unknown. (Right) For the nation's centennial celebration in 1976, Muni gave car #1170 a patriotic livery of red, white and bue, and for this occasion, the number 1776. ***Stindt photos.***

First LRVs to arrive in San Francisco #1220 and #1221, October 22, 1977. They were used in extensive tests. Returned to the maker, Boeing Vertol for modification. They returned as #1212 and #1213. *Muni photo.*

Muni had no definite plans as to what type of passenger vehicle they would use in the subway. In early 1968 they came up with the German DuWag 100 passenger articulated car with four trucks. With a "buy American" wave sweeping the country, this plan went out the window. The Public Utilities Commission then teamed up with the City of Boston to purchase 230 new street cars. This agreement took place, August 23, 1972. Eighty cars would be for San Francisco allotment.

In mid-1972, a $44 million transit improvement program was approved by the San Francisco Board of Supervisors. Tracks would be rerailed on all five Muni street surface lines. Included in the funding would be a Metro Shop Center to be built on the old Elkton shop site along with car storage.

Also in 1972 the United States Department of Transportation's Urban Mass Transportation Administration, which became known as UMTA, enacted a program to develop a Light Rail Vehicle that would replace the PCC street car. The LRV would have a modern look with quick acceleration on city streets and have a speed of 50 miles per hour on private right-of-way or in subways. It was hoped the design would have an appeal for new systems to various cities nationwide. UMTA was joined by eight transit operators and two design firms, which included San Francisco's Muncipal Railway and Boston's Massachusetts Bay Transportation Authority.

UMTA called for bids. The award went to Boeing-Vertol on February 15, 1973 for the 230 Light Rail Vehicles. The two unit articulated three-truck cars would be built at the Philadelphia, PA plant. Each would be 71 feet long with passenger seating of 68. A 9.1 mile loop test track was constructed at Pueblo, Colorado, where cars were given exhaustive tests. The first unit off the assembly line came in September, 1974. With several others, the tests proved that much upgrading had to be accomplished to adhere to specifications.

In June, 1974, San Francisco ordered an additional twenty cars to make the total one hundred (Boston's order went to 175 for their "green" lines B-C-D-E).

Meanwhile, work was proceeding on the construction of BART. With endless delays the first BART train with press radio and TV personel aboard arrived at the Embarcadero Subway station, San Francisco from Oakland on August 10, 1973. Local passenger service between Montgomery and Daly City was inaugurated on November 8, 1973, with full transbay service including the Embarcadero Station commencing September 16, 1974. The Muni subway was in place, but no cars were available for the operation.

The contract for reconstruction of the West Portal entrance to a station was awarded May 18, 1976. It would include 350-foot loading and unloading platforms with entrance and egress on the west end. To cut down on street car traffic while this construction work was going on along with rerailing the tunnel tracks, the "M" line was discontinued from January 13, 1974 to December 20, 1978.

Elkton shops, orginally built in 1907, were closed down on May 31, 1977. Work began on demolition of the old building and the start of the new Metro Shop and yard tracks. The new facility was formally dedicated on June 1, 1979.

The first LRV's #1220 and 1221, arrived in San Francisco, October 22, 1977. The cars, with trolley poles, came in for extensive tests. A preview ride took place on January 31, 1978 between the Embarcadero and Castro stations and return. The ride included the city's politicos, press, radio, TV, Boeing Vertol representatives and a very interesting personality, James. J.

Car #1040 fresh out of the paint shop is sporting the new Landor Sunset Glow and California Poppy colors, October 28, 1978, as the car heads into the Geneva car barn. ***Stindt photo.***

(Above) Prior to the arrival of the LRVs #1008 was equipped with a pantograph for overhead wire testing in 1977. In 1980 it was assigned to Repair Car status still retaining the number 1008. ***Will Whittaker photo.*** **(Below) In the late 1950s Muni #130 became a "wrecker" to haul disabled cars to the barn. Renumbered 0131. Photo shows unit at west end of Twin Peaks tunnel in late 1960s. Restored to street car status in 1983 and joined Festival car fleet in blue and yellow livery.** ***Tom Gray photo.***

O'Brien, 85, who was named the honorary conductor. Mr. O'Brien, a former Muni conductor, had retired after 42 years of service and was the conductor of the first street car to go through the Twin Peaks tunnel in 1918. The cars were returned to the builder for modification. They returned as #1212 and #1213. The delivery of the LRV's finally got under way in the Spring of 1978, with #1222 the first to arrive. The order of 100 cars was complete in the Spring of 1980.

The day finally came for the initial start of the LRV cars, such taking place on April 23, 1979, with a shuttle service from West Portal to Balboa Park on the "K" line. Meanwhile, testing of the cars continued in the subway. November 12, 1979, saw a bad accident occur when one unit rolled into another west of the Van Ness station. Cars #1222A and 1252B were totalled and scrapped. No 1222B and 1252A became a new 1222. It was not until 1982 when a new 1252 was delivered from Boeing Vertol (ex Boston #3565, which had not been delivered to the Boston Company).

During the lengthy time in phasing in the LRV's, the maintenance of the PCC cars took a decided drop. To keep going, Muni gave 30 of the PCC units a good overhaul and came out in yet another new Muni color, that of Landor Sunset Glow and California Poppy colors. Even with these rejuvenated cars, the Muni many times was pressed for serviceable PCC cars and had to substitute buses to the disgust of the patrons.

In 1979, the Muni came out with a five year plan. In essence the phases of this plan were as follows: Phase One, LRV's on "N" line; Phase Two, LRV's on "K" and "L" lines and Phase Three: LRV's on the "J" and "M" lines. The five year plan also included a future extension of the "J" line from Church and 30th via San Jose Avenue to the Muni Metro Center at Geneva; the surfacing of the Market Street Subway cars, by turning south under the Embarcadero and coming to the surface between Mission and Folsom Street. The "J" and "M" lines would be extended on new tracks along the Embarcadero, King, to Fourth Street Southern Pacific Station to serve peninsula commuters and also to continue into the Mission Bay project. A storage facility would also be included in the Mission Bay area. A new line known as the "F" line would operate from Castro on Market, Steuart to just short of Mission, to new Embarcadero tracks to Fisherman's wharf area.

Also, in 1979, the Muni received a federal grant of $27.6 million part of which was designated to extend the "M" line from Plymouth and Broad, on Broad to San Jose Avenue to Balboa Park station at Geneva. This was completed on August 30, 1980.

On February 19, 1980, the "N" line commenced with LRV service including the Market Street subway, Monday through Friday, with PCC cars on the weekends using the Market Street surface tracks. June 11, 1980, saw subway service via LRV to St. Francis Circle on the "K" line with the PCC cars assigned to a "K" and "L" shuttle service between Phelan Loop on the "K" line, to the Zoo at 47th Avenue and Wawona on the "L" line. Connection for downtown passengers was made at West Portal. This service operated Monday through Friday. On the weekends full PCC service as before. The "K"and "L" PCC shuttle ended December 16, 1980 and Monday-Friday LRV service took over the following day with the "K" line extended to Balboa Park Station via Ocean Avenue. All lines still used PCC cars on the week-ends. The Phelan Loop was abandoned on March 17, 1981, with PCC cars on the weekends continuing on Ocean to San Jose Avenue to the Geneva car barn where a loop was made inside the facility. Monday-Friday LRV service began on the "J" line, June 17, 1981.

The end of the PCC car era came Sunday evening, September 19, 1982 when the last one operated and the LRV's took over completely every day of the week. The "K" and "L" lines, on weekends account reconstruction of the Forest Hill station in the Twin Peaks tunnel, became a shuttle between Balboa Park on the "K" line to the Zoo on the "L" line. Buses were used downtown over Twin Peaks from the West Portal transfer point. The "M" line was total bus operation.

With the Forest Hill station project completed, full LRV service, each day, took effect on all lines, November 20, 1982, five long years after the first LRV arrived in San Francisco.

As to the disposition of the PCC cars, which numbered 104, (one was totalled with a collision with with a truck in 1972 (#1102), twelve went to museums or other use (1014, 1016, 1030, 1033, 1039, 1118, 1121, 1134, 1135, 1146, 1150, and 1159), three retained for San Francisco's summer festival car service (1006, 1040, 1128 as 1702), one a repair car (1008), one stored at Geneva (1108) and 43 were trucked to Pier 70 where they were stored for future use on the planned "F" line. During the week of May 18, 1987 they were moved to a new location in the Pier 72 area, at the foot of 23rd Street. The rest were scrapped (see roster for details).

The new LRV's were immediately accepted and patronage grew by leaps and bounds, so additional cars were sorely needed. Boston had incurred numerous problems with the LRV's they received and did not accept thirty-six in their order of 175. One had already come to San Francisco to replace the wrecked units and numbered #1252. San Francisco okayed thirty cars providing a number of modifications were made, which Beoing-Vetrol agreed to do. The remaining five cars were scrapped by Boeing for parts. The first to arrive was #1300 on February 2, 1983 and the last #1329 on February 15, 1984. Of interest, as of January 12, 1990, Boston has retired 28 LRV's leaving 116 operable.

After many months in construction, the new $4 million three-story Metro Center Annex and the new Geneva car house across the street with its modern paint and body shops along with wash racks and storage for 53 LRV cars, was dedicated on May 8, 1985. In the winter months two tracks are available to store the Festival cars. The old office building at Geneva and San Jose Avenue, directly in front of the Geneva facility, that was built in 1901 by the old San Francisco and San Mateo Railroad, was left intact and remained in use as an office building, until the earthquake, October 17, 1989, when it suffered structural damage. The "M" line cars outer terminous was changed to loop through Geneva yard.

As seen from the mezzanine, this is a view of the Muni level in the Market Street subway's Embarcadero Station. One of the four stations shared with BART, which runs on the lower level, it was not in the original plans. Its $40 million cost was financed through arrangements by the City and County of San Francisco. Other joint use stations: Montgomery, Powell and Civic Center. Sole Muni use: Van Ness, Church and Castro stations in the subway. ***Muni photo.***

LRV units #1272 and #1244 glide along inbound having just passed St Francis Circle into West Portal, on the "M" line, June 27, 1989. ***Stindt photo.***

Operating expenses continued to mount in 1988 and with the city in a financial bind and Muni losses ever higher, Muni was faced with another fare increase. Such took place on August 1, 1988, when the fare went from 75 cents to 85 cents and cable car fare from $1.50 to $2.00. Of interest the following are the fares charged by Muni since its beginning in 1912. The grand nickel fare that lasted for 32 years went to 7 cents October 15, 1944. Since then as follows:

May 20, 1946	10 cents or 8 1/3 token rate
January 26, 1949	Straight 10 cent fare
June 1, 1952	To 15 cents
June 30, 1969	To 20 cents; 5 cent seniors, 25 cents cable cars
August 31, 1970	To 25 cents
April 1, 1980	To 50 cents; 50 cents cable cars
April 1, 1982	To 60 cents; $1.00 cable cars
January 1, 1986	To 75 cents; 15 cents seniors, $1.50 cable cars
August 1, 1988	To 85 cents; $2.00 cable cars, $1.00 valid transfer

In 1970, the California Legislature created the Metropolitan Transportation Commission (MTC) charging the commission with developing a regional transportation plan to help map new transit lines and highways. MTC immediately became responsible for allocating funds disbursed pursuant to the Federal Surface Transportation Act of 1964. In 1971, the State Transportation Development Act emerged, broadening MTC's authority to include responsibility for directly allocating or approving the spending of state as well as federal funds. MTC currently allocates nearly a billion dollars each year of local, state and federal funds for transit, roads and airports. The area served by MTC includes nine counties; Sonoma, Napa, Solano, Marin, Contra Costa, Alameda, San Francisco, San Mateo and Santa Clara. In this area are 23 separate transit operators receiving funds of which San Francisco Municipal Railway is one. The Muni is very dependent on MTC allocations as can be seen by the following figures; for the year 1989, the Muni carried 245 million passengers who paid $75 million into the fare box, far short of the $235 million required to operate the system. Local taxes made up $105 million with MTC directing $37 million from state assistance, $8 million from federal funding and other revenue $10 million. Originally there was a rule that 33% of total operating cost had to be from the fare box before state and federal funds could be allocated. However, this rule was amended to include in the 33%, local funding, i.e., city taxes, so the 33% criteria can now be easily met.

The MTC has approved capital grants for the following Muni street car extensions or new lines in recent years: (1) "J" line extension from 30th and Church to San Jose and Geneva Avenues (work commenced January 17, 1989) (2) Continuation of Market Street tracks from Fremont to Steuart, thence right ¾ block toward Mission Street, then left through the Muni bus turn around area, across Embarcadero south auto lane, thence left along former Belt line tracks to Fisherman's wharf area, west on Jefferson, looping on Jones to Beach and return to Embarcadero. (3) An extension to bring the Market Street subway to the surface between Mission and Folsom then south along the Embarcadero, west on King to the CalTrain station at 4th Street. Also approved, with work already in progress, is relaying rail on Market Street between Fremont and Duboce and new rail between Duboce and Castro with a Noe-17th-Castro turn around. The work between Fremont and 11th was scheduled for the summer months of 1988-89. The first phase between 3rd and 8th commenced May 9, 1988 and completed on November 23rd. The second phase, Fremont to 3rd and 8th to 11th, began March 1, 1989 and completed on October 23rd. A special ribbon cutting program and free historic street car rides were planned for November 21, 1989, but was marred by an activist march that tied up traffic.

Along with the MTC, the Regional Transit Association of the Bay Area (RTA) was formed in 1979 by six of the largest transit systems; AC Transit, BART, Muni, Golden Gate Bridge Highway and Transportation District, San Mateo County Transit and Santa Clara County Transit. In recent years Contra County Transit Authority has also joined along with the participation of Peninsula CalTrains. It is the purpose of this group, consisting of member system general managers, to deal with service coordination by substantially reducing duplication of similar efforts at each RTA property in marketing efforts, purchasing, various phases of public information and career development programs for transit employees. Muni works closely with this group, so as to provide smooth connections at transfer points and ease commuter traffic jams.

On May 9, 1989, the city Public Utilities Commission held a public hearing on Muni's plan to request from the Federal government, $45.2 million to purchase 40 new type street cars with a planned delivery in six years. The new cars would be longer than the present LRV's and with a greater seating capacity. They would be used on the "J" line extension, the new Mission Bay commercial and residential line, and improving existing service. The Muni also stated that in less than ten years of service the present LRV's have started to "fall to pieces." Boeing-Vertol, builder of the cars, has long since gone out of business and foreign manufacturers of various components also have left the transit field. There is no question that the Muni is hard-pressed to keep the present fleet going, so the program presented for the new cars is a necessity. Two wrecked cars #1212 (1212A-1255B) and #1294 (1294B and 1297A) were scrapped in July, 1989. #1212B-1255A became #1255 and #1294A and #1297B became #1297.

On Thursday, October 17, 1989, at 5:04 p.m. an earthquake of 7.1 magnitude struck the San Francisco Bay Area. The epicenter was located 70 miles south of San Francisco near the community of Loma Prieta in the Santa Cruz district. The devastation was enormous; $6 billion in damage, 62 killed and over 3,000 injured. A 50-foot section of the Bay Bridge fell on the lower deck and in Oakland a mile of elevated freeway (I-880) collapsed on the lower roadway. This is where most casualties occurred. The Embarcadero elevated freeway was judged unsafe and closed. The Marina area where the 1915 Exposition was held was badly hit. The San Francisco Municipal Railway and Bay Area Rapid Transit (BART) fortunately suffered little or no damage, but were shut down account of power outages. The Muni on the following day ran their "J" and "N" lines short of the subway at Duboce and Church and the "K," "L," and "M" lines ran only to the Van Ness subway station and switched back manually. The next day all operation was returned to normal. With less auto traffic into the city, BART and Muni patronage jumped considerably. However, there was one casualty, the old three-story Geneva office building built by the San Mateo and San Francisco Railroad in 1901 was severally damaged. At this writing (June, 1990) it has not been determined as to repair the structure or tear it down. The Bay Bridge was repaired and back in business a month later with a walk tour and "welcome back" program, Thursday, November 16, 1989 (9,195 purchased the $6 tickets for the walk.) Auto traffic resumed the following evening at 11:18 p.m.

On election day, November 7, 1989, the voters of San Francisco approved a half-cent sales tax increase. 60% would go for transit improvements and over a 20-year period, would generate $540 million. This would greatly assist funding for the Mission Bay Metro extension, the "F" line Embarcadero line and studies for the proposed Geary subway. The proposal calls for plans to operate from outer Geary Street, enter a subway as it nears downtown then down Third Street, surface and connect with the Mission Bay extension at King Street.

With refurbished PCC cars available in Philadelphia and in better condition than Muni's PCC's stored in the Pier 72 area, transit officials met with Southeastern Pennsylvania Transit Authority (SEPTA) heads in Philadelphia, February 21, 1990. Muni concluded an agreement to purchase twenty PCC type cars. One would be shipped to San Francisco as soon as practical. This unit would then be shopped and determination made as to whether to retain the motors and regauge (Philadelphia has a different gauge) or use the motors and trucks from cars now stored at the Pier 72 site. As of June 1, 1990 this car has not arrived. When the program of shopping is complete the cars would be used on the "F" line service on Market Street.

Also, under consideration, the Muni in September, 1990 will advertise for bids on 40 new LRV cars with an option for an additional ten. Bids to be received in November.

As this book goes to the printer, June, 1990, the five electric street car lines J-K-L-M-N are firmly entrenched in the city's transportation system. In addition, three new lines are in various stages of reality. The two-mile "J" line extension will be completed in late 1990 or early 1991. The new Castro-Market-Embarcadero "F" line is scheduled to begin in 1993 from Castro to the East Bay Terminal and a year later to the Ferry Terminal. It will necessitate new track construction from Duboce on Market to 17th to begin in 1991 along with track repair from 11th to 12th. Replace rail on Market from 12th to Duboce is scheduled for 1992 and to start the extension from Fremont on Market to Steuart to near Mission and Embarcadero in 1993. The line will eventually extend along The Embarcadero to the Fisherman's Wharf area. In the years 1992-1995 new construction will bring the subway to surface on the Embarcadero between Mission and Folsom, then new track along a private right-of-way to King Street to 7th in the Mission Bay project. A new LRV maintenance facility is planned at the old Southern Pacific roundhouse site bounded by 16th, Mariposa and the SP tracks. There may be some delay account the fate of the Embarcadero freeway which has been closed since the October 17, 1989 earthquake. The mayor and supervisors want it torn down and a new underground expressway built in its place. The deadline is August 1, 1990, to find funds for the ambitious project. If the expressway is okayed, Muni's expansion plans would be delayed, but remain intact.

Muni's street car system and the extensive planning for its future is a far cry from 40 years ago when a consortium of bus, tire, and gasoline interests attempted to buy out and abolish all street car lines in the U.S.A. in favor of their motor buses - and almost succeeded. As the flanged wheel on fixed rail approaches the century mark in the City by the Bay, the electric street car remains the backbone of San Francisco's vast transportation network.

CHAPTER 5

SAN FRANCISCO MUNICIPAL RAILWAY

THE ELECTRIC STREET CARS

The following listing will show all the street cars that were owned and operated by the San Francisco Muncipal Railway from the beginning of the railway in 1912 to the present time. Not included are those cars taken over from the Market Street Railway in 1944 nor outside cars obtained for Festival car service on Market Street in recent years. The compliation indicates that there were 514 street cars in service at one time or other.

1-20

Type "A." the first of the Muni street cars. Built by W.L. Holman Company, San Francisco and delivered in mid-December, 1912 and into 1913. Most were ready for operation when Muni began its service on Geary Street, December 28, 1912. The cars costing $7,700 each had the "California" type design; open sections each end, center section enclosed. The open ends had longitudinal seating on one side, cross seating on the other. The center section, cross seating both sides. All seats rattan. Total seating 48. Designed by transit consultant Bion J. Arnold, the cars became known as "Arnold" cars. The cars were narrower, 8'6" compared with customary 9' cars. After arrival of type "B" cars the "Arnold" cars were basically assigned to the "F" line where they stayed until the line went trolly bus, January 19, 1951. The late Gilbert Kneiss, director of the Pacific Coast Chapter, Railway & Locomotive Historical society and myself, then chairman of the chapter, prevailed upon the Muni to save car #1. When the Geary barn was converted to trolley bus operation, car #1 was brought to Pier 25 along San Francisco's waterfront for further storage, July 30, 1959. Three years later it was brought to Elkton shops for overhaul and restored to its former appearance for Muni's 50th anniversary, which took place in October, 1962. #1 today (1990) is part of the Muni Festival car fleet.

Car #5 sports the Muni gray drab paint scheme in the year 1940 at the outer "C" terminus of 33rd & California. ***Guido collection.***

21-43

Type "A." With the Holman company broke and going out of business with delivery of car #20, the same contract was taken over by Union Iron Works, San Francisco, which later became Bethlehem Shipyard. The 23 cars were delivered by June 25, 1913. By mid-1920's all cars #1-43 had their end sections enclosed and longitudinal seating placed on one side of the center section account the narrow aisle. Besides the "A" line at the outset, the "Arnold" cars also saw service on occasions on other Geary lines, the "H" line and "M" line shuttle service. The eclipse fenders (cow-catchers) remained with the cars until their demise in 1951. All received the blue and yellow paint decor in 1940's and just about all received the cream and green with the wing design in the late 1940's. With the exception of car #1, all were scrapped in 1951 upon the demise of the "F" line.

Car #35 in the Muni blue and yellow decor near Geary on Stockton in the year 1939. ***Guido collection.***

44-168

Type "B." With new Muni lines being rapidly established in the mid-1910's, Muni ordered 125 cars of the "California" type from the Jewett Car Company, Newark, Ohio at a cost of $7,000 each. Delivery began June 25, 1913. By 1925, the end sections with its cross seating had been enclosed. The center section retained the longitudinal seating of the rather hard sitting veneer wood composition. The cars of this design became known as "iron monsters." Used on all Market Street lines along with the cross town "H" line. Car #50 was destroyed by fire while in the Geary barn paint shop, November 27, 1934. In the late 1940's all cars of this design #44-213 received safety bars on the ends in place of the fenders (cow-catchers). Cars #150-213 received folding entrance doors around this time, with the doors coming from scrapped ex-Market Street Railway cars. Car #130 went to "wrecker" status #0131 in early 1960's. It went back to original (#130) appearance in the blue and yellow livery in late 1983 to be retained in Festival car service. #162 to Orange Empire Railway Museum, Perris, California, September 21, 1958. All others scrapped 1952-1958.

(Above) Car #55 at the Geary car barn in 1915. Note open end sections. *Smallwood collection.*
(Below) Car #138 at the "N" line terminus at Judah and La Playa, March 1940. The end sections were enclosed in the mid 1920's. *Will Whittaker photo.*

169-188

Type "K." Built by Bethlehem Shipyard, San Francisco, at a cost of $16,500 each. With a seating capacity of 50 the cars were essentially the same as the class "B" cars. Delivered with enclosed sections July through November 1923. Assigned to all Market lines and crosstown "H" line. With okay by the city voters in 1954 for one-man cars, these cars with all others of this type (44-213) were phased out. They were not altered for one-man operation, but stayed two-man until the end. Last to go to the scrap dock was #186, March 11, 1959. The following were saved for museum purposes: #171 to San Diego Historical Society, Perris, CA, 1959; #178 to Bay Area Electric Ass'n, Rio Vista, CA, March 6, 1959 (used as a Festival car on Market Street 1983, 1984, 1985).

Car #184 ambles along Union Street inbound with its destination the East Bay Terminal downtown in the year 1946. ***Guido collection.***

189-213

Type "L." Built by St. Louis Car Company at a cost of $19,200 each. 15 were delivered June 15, 1927, the rest by March 15, 1928. Same specifications as Type "B" and "K." These 25 cars were acquired for the newly built "N" line, which went into operation in the Sunset District, October 21, 1928. Also, assigned to any Market line and crosstown "H." To spruce up the cars from their dull gray appearance, the Muni adopted the California colors of blue and gold (yellow) in time for the Golden Gate International Exposition held at man-made Treasure Island in San Francisco Bay during the years 1939-1940. All of the cars #1-213 received this paint decor. In the late 1940's the cream and green livery with the side wings became the standard color. With the one-man PCC cars taking over, all of these cars were scrapped in 1957-1958.

Car #203 swings from Junipero Serra into Ocean on a summer day in 1949. Note safety bar has been installed along with entrance folding doors. ***Tom Gray collection.***

301-329

Type "G." These 29 cars (#1-29) came into Muni ownership when the Presidio & Ferries Railroad was purchased, December 11, 1913. Previously, after the earthquake and fire of April 18, 1906, the Presidio & Ferries replaced their cable cars with these single truck electric cars purchased from United Railroads. Most had been built before the turn-of-the-century. These cars were retired November 22, 1922 being replaced by new cars (see 351-371). All were sold August 7, 1923 for $125 each, except five which became Muni service cars #C-2 to C-6. #C-4 (ex-Muni #317 and P&F #28) went to a farm near Pescadero, San Mateo County in 1946. In 1965 to Bay Area Electric Ass'n at Rio Vista, where it sits derelict today (1990).

Car #308 at an unknown location the "E" line in the decade of the 1910's.

351-370

Type "J." Built by American Car Company at a cost of $11,500 each. They were small center entrance cars with a seating of 32. Delivered November 1, 1922. Replaced the 301-329 on the "E" line. They were at times used on the "F" line and the short-lived "O" line. When the "E" line ended its street car operation on June 8, 1947 in favor of trolley buses, the cars were soon scrapped. The cars kept their fenders until the end. None received the blue and yellow colors, retaining the Muni gray until their demise.

Car #368 arrives at the North Ferry Terminal in the late 1930's. ***Bert Ward photo.***

371 Type "J-L." Built by A. Meister & Co., Sacramento, for $15,000. Delivered as car #200, March 28, 1921 as a trial car for the "E" lines. Okayed and used as a prototype for 20 additional cars. Renumbered #371 in 1923. Sold for scrap, May 28, 1958.

Car #371 was a little different from the other "dinkies" as to its front roof design and the route destination roller was over the right front window instead of on the roof. At the Ferry Terminal year 1940. *Guido collection.*

1001-1005

Type "C." With the development of the modern streamline PCC type street car in 1936, the Muni placed an order with the St. Louis Car Company for five cars in early 1939. They were not a true PCC car as the city charter did not allow patent royalty payments, so various alterations were made. They were dubbed the "Magic Carpet" cars. The cars seating 60 cost $22,400 each. They arrived October 31, 1939 in the newly established blue and gold (yellow) paint scheme. They were assigned to any of the Market lines and gained immediate favorable reaction from the riding public. World War II precluded any new car orders for the duration. In 1954, the city voters okayed the one-man car, so these cars along with Type "D" (1006-1015) were changed from two-man, double-end, to one-man, single-end. The cars had a few operations quirks, such as an awkward hand control system. All were scrapped in 1959-1960, except car #1003, which went to the Bay Area Electric Ass'n museum at Rio Vista.

Art Lloyd was on hand to snap car #1004 at the Ferry Loop, April 25, 1946.

1006-1015

Type "D," nick-named "Torpedoes."Built by the St. Louis Car Company in 1948. Delivered with the new cream and green decor and side wing design. As two-man cars they had walkover seats with a capacity of 59. In 1954, changed to one-man, single-end operation. All PCC car service ended September 19, 1982 with the Light Rail Vehicles taking over. #1006 retained as a Festival car and #1008 converted to a Repair Car. #1014 to a Museum, Sydney, Australia, May 8, 1987. All others stored or scrapped. See roster page.

Car #1007 pauses at the outer terminal of the "N" line at La Playa and Judah Streets in the year 1950. ***Guido collection.***

1016-1040 PCC class. Built by the St. Louis Car Company in 1951. Muni wanted the cars like type "D," but with builders winding down their PCC construction, Muni had to accept the standard model with center exit doors, seating 58. The center door was the entrance for two-man operation until changed to one-man in 1954. This was the last order for PCC cars, so car #1040 has the distinction of the last built. This car retained for Festival car service. Both #1038 and #1040 received the Landor Sunset glow and California poppy colors when shopped in 1978. With PCC service ending, September 19, 1982, the cars were either scrapped or placed in storage or donated. See roster page.

Car #1040, the last PCC car built in the U.S.A. rolls up Market Street, May, 1974. ***Stindt photo***

1101-1166 PCC Type. These cars were built by the St. Louis Car Company in 1946 for the St. Louis Public Service Inc. In 1957 these 53-seat cars were leased and subsequently purchased by Muni in 1964. These cars would phase out the remaining two-man "iron monsters." Before leaving St. Louis, each of the cars was refurbished, back-up controls installed and repainted to the green and cream decor. They were then placed on railroad flat cars for transport to San Francisco. They were well received. In 1963, another modification of the paint livery took place. Account of the ads covering the wing design, about half the cars had a larger cream band placed around the car with the wings removed. In the late 1970's with constant delays in getting the new LRV's into service, the PCC's, with little maintenance, began to falter. 24 were completely shopped and came out with the Landor Sunset glow, white and orange poppy color. When the PCC operation ended, September 19, 1982, the cars were either scrapped, placed in storage or donated. See roster page.

(Below) Car #1120 speeds up outer Market Street, June, 1974, ***Stindt photo.***

Car* #1129 emerges from Twin Peaks tunnel recently reconstructed with platforms for the new LRV service. Year 1980.** ***Stindt photo.

1167-1170 PCC Type. Built by the St. Louis Car Company in 1946 for the St. Louis Public Service, Inc. Leased by Muni in 1962 and purchased two years later. During the country's bi-centennial celebration in 1976, Car #1170 was patriotically painted red, white and blue and renumbered 1776 for the occasion. In 1978, all four of these cars received heavy repairs and painted the colorful Landor, red, white and orange livery. The #1776 went back to #1170. When the PCC's ended September 19, 1982, #1167 was scrapped but the other three were stored at Pier 70. In May, 1987, with other stored PCC cars were moved to Pier 72.

Car #1170 trundles up outer Market Street, May 9, 1974. The car would receive the "Centennial" paint scheme in 1976 and two years later the Landor California poppy and Sunset glow colors. ***Stindt photo.***

1180-1189

PCC Type. Built by the St. Louis Car Company in 1946 for the Kansas City Public Service, Inc. Sold to Toronto Transportation Commission in 1957. With the Duboce, Church, 17th Street detour account the Market Street subway construction, extra cars were needed. As these were available, Muni purchased them in 1974 and gave them numbers 1180-1189. The cars remained in their Canadian maroon and buff colors except the lower panel was given a coat of red paint. They were 8'4'' wide, narrower than the standard PCC cars. They were not popular with operators. Car #1184 almost made service, but like #1185 never did. All scrapped in 1979, except #1183 which went to the Illinois museum at Union, February, 1980.

Ex Kansas City, ex Toronto, Canada, now Muni #1183 ready to turn off Market into Duboce, June, 1976. The 2nd hand cars were bought in 1974, but lasted only five years. This car ended a better fate going to a museum in Illinois. ***Stindt photo.***

1190

PCC Type. Same details as #1180-1189, except built in 1947. Phased out in 1979. To the Bay Area Electric Railway Ass'n museum at Rio Vista in April, 1980.

Car #1190 outbound on the "N" line on upper Market Street before turning at Duboce. Arriving in 1974 the unit only operated on the Muni for five years. These cars were not a favorite of the operators. To museum Rio Vista, CA. ***Stindt photo.***

1200-1299 Articulated Light Rail Vehicle. The cars were a development of a design established by the U.S. Dept. of Transportation's Urban Mass Transportation Administration (UMTA). A contract went to Boeing-Vertol on February 15, 1973 for 230 cars; 80 for San Francisco and 150 for Boston. The 68 seat cars would be built at the Philadelphia plant. In June 1974, Muni ordered 20 additional cars, Boston 25 for a new total of 275. A test track was installed at Pueblo, Colorado. Numerous "bugs" developed, so the first cars #1220 and #1221 did not arrive San Francisco until October 22, 1977. There were a number of tests and the cars were sent back for further modifications. They returned a year later as #1212 and #1213. Finally they began to arrive in goodly numbers in the Spring of 1980, but it took two years more before they were all on the property. They were unique for San Francisco as they had operator controls for high/low steps at all entrances for either street or subway platform loading. There were continuous tests before the cars were phased in on all five lines. One was a disaster. On November 12, 1979, one car rolled into another in the subway, which totalled #1222A and #1252B. #1222B and #1252A became #1222. A new #1252 was delivered by Boeing Vertol in 1982. The day finally came when LRV service took over completely on September 19, 1982 and the PCC cars came to an end, almost ten years since the order was placed for LRV cars. During July, 1989, account accidents Muni scrapped LRV's #1212 (1212A and #1255B) and #1294 (1294B and 1297A). Numbers 1212B and 1255A became #1255 and numbers 1294A and 1297B became #1297. In operation today (1990).

Car #1217 and #1257 have just emerged from the Twin Peaks tunnel to head out to Balboa Park station via the "M" line in the year 1984. ***Tom Gray photo.***

1300-1329 Built by Boeing-Vertol in 1982. Boston had incurred numerous problems with the LRV's, so cancelled 36 cars in their order of 175. Muni was badly in need of additional cars, as the subway LRV service had increased patronage by leaps and bounds. With many modifications Muni placed an order for 30 of the cars that became available. The first, #1300, arrived on February 2, 1983 and the last was delivered February 15, 1984. Note - of the six remaining Boston cars, one came to the Muni as #1252 in 1982, the other five were scrapped for parts. In operation today (1990).

LRV # **1329 rolls along Ocean Avenue inbound, March 20, 1984.** ***Muni photo.***

SAN FRANCISCO MUNICIPAL RAILWAY
ROSTER
ELECTRIC STREET CARS

Numbers	Builder	Date	Remarks - Disposition
1-20	W. L. Holman	1912-13	Sold for scrap in 1951, except #1-see note.
21-43	Union Iron Works	1913	Sold for scrap in 1951.
44-168	Jewett Car Co.	1913	#50 destroyed by fire, November 27, 1934. See note for others.
169-188	Bethlehem, San Francisco	1923	See note.
189-213	St. Louis Car Co.	1927-28	See note.
301-329	Hammond	?	Ex Presidio & Ferries. Purchased 1913. 19 to Market Str. Ry. (1923) Others see note.
351-370	American Car Co.	1922	Sold for scrap 1948, except 358,368 in 1947.
371	A. Meister Co.	1921	Ex #200. To #371 in 1922. Sold for scrap, 1948.
1001-1005	St. Louis Car Co.	1939	Magic Carpet cars. See note.
1006-1015	St. Louis Car Co.	1948	See note.
1016-1040	St. Louis Car Co.	1951	See note.
1101-1166	St. Louis Car Co.	1946	#1102 wrecked 1972 and scrapped. Others see note.
1167-1170	St. Louis Car Co.	1946	See note.
1180-1189	St. Louis Car Co.	1946	#1184 & #1185 never used. #1183 to Illinois Ry Museum (1908) Others scrapped 1979.
1190	St. Louis Car Co.	1947	To Western Ry. Museum, Rio Vista, CA (1980).
1200-1221	Boeing Vertol	1977-78	Light Rail Vehicle (LRV) Metro cars. All in operation 1990, except #1212 see note.
1222	Boeing Vertol Co.	1978	#1222A wrecked 11-12-79. Section B and section #1252A made into #1222.
1223-1251	Boeing Vertol	1979	LRV - all on active roster 1990.
1st1252	Boeing Vertol	1979	#1252B wrecked 11-12-79. Section #1252A to #1222A.
2nd1252	Boeing Vertol	1982	LRV - Ex Boston #3565, built not delivered. 1982 to Muni.
1253-1299	Boeing Vertol	1980	LRV - All on active roster 1990, except #1294. See note.
1300-1329	Boeing Vertol	1982	LRV - all in operation 1990.

NOTES

#1 prevailed upon by the Railway & Locomotive Historical Society to save for museum purposes. 1959 to Pier 25, San Francisco for storage. Started to sink through rotted pilings. Back to Elkton Shops and restored to original appearance in time for Muni 50th year celebration, October, 1962. Retained as a Festival car.

44-213 Scrapped in 1952: 46, 56, 65, 67, 72, 79, 80, 82, 87, 92-94, 99, 102, 105, 109, 112, 121, 128, 131, 134, 137, 144, 149. For reasons unknown Muni renumbered many of the remaining cars into numbers as shown below in paranthesis. Cars were thusly scrapped with number last shown in paranthesis.

Scrapped in 1955: 48 (124-74), 62 (80-71), 77 (70), 96, 98, 115 (3rd 72), 119 (3rd 73) and 129 (75).

Scrapped in 1956: 59 (102), 75, 76, 123, 138, 141, 147.

Scrapped in 1957: 44 (144), 45 (137), 47 (131), 49 (121), 51 (112), 52 (109), 53 (79), 54 (134), 55 (93), 57 (92-75), 58 (128), 60 (149), 61 (82), 63 (94), 64 (87), 66 (72-115), 68 (99), 69 (105), 70 (77), 71 (80), 73 (119), 74 (124), 78, 81, 83-86, 88-91, 95, 97, 100, 101, 103, 104, 106-108, 110, 111, 113, 114, 116-118, 120, 122, 125 (142), 126, 127, 132, 133, 135, 136, 139, 140, 142 (125), 143, 145, 146, 148, 150, 151, 160, 164, 165, 170, 175, 180, 182, 191, 194, 200, 211.

301-329 United Railroads sold these cars to Presidio & Ferries in 1907 and were numbered 1-29. To Muni in 1913 and renumbered 301-329. In 1929, 19 resold to Market Street Railway for parts. Six scrapped. Four to service cars, 323, 317, 303 and 311 which became C-3, C-4, C-5, C-6. Scrapped 1940, except C-4. Sold to a rancher at Pescadero, 1946. Donated 1965 to Bay Area Electric Ass'n museum, Rio Vista, in derelict condition. Not restored (1990). Originally United Railroads #755, thence P&F #28, Muni #317, thence C-4.

1001-1005 Scrapped in 1959-1960, except #1003 to Western Railway Museum, Rio Vista (1960).

1006-1015 #1006 retained as a Festival car. #1008 converted to LRV Repair car in 1981. #1014 to museum, Australia (5-8-87). Scrapped 1983; #1012, 1013. Held for reserve stored outside Pier 72 area, San Francisco (1990); 1007, 1009, 1010, 1011, 1015.

1016-1040 #1040 retained as a Festival car. #1016 to Western Railway museum, Rio Vista (1983), #1030 to Illinois museum (1983), #1033 and #1039 to Orange Empire Railway museum, Perris, CA. (1983). Sold for junk 1982; 1017, 1018, 1019, 1020, 1021, 1022, 1025, 1029, 1032, 1036, 1037. Held for reserve outside Pier 72 area; 1023, 1024, 1026, 1027, 1028, 1031, 1034, 1035, 1038, (1990).

1101-1170 #1102 wrecked 1972 and scrapped. #1108 stored at Geneva car barn (1990). #1128 to #1702 retained as Festival car. #1118 sold to Mike Lands, Sherwood, Oregon-to Glenwood (8-28-81); #1121 to Pacific Southwest museum, San Diego (5-3-88); #1134 and # 1135 to Nevada State Railroad museum, Carson City, NV (March 1983); #1146 to Western Railway museum for transfer to Kansas City, MO. (June, 1981), #1156 to Western Railway museum, Rio Vista (March, 1983), #1164 To Wisconsin Electric Railway Society (March, 1983) to Nat. Museum of Transport, St. Louis (June, 1989)

Sold for scrap 1981: 1104, 1107, 1112, 1114, 1116, 1117, 1119, 1120, 1126, 1129, 1132, 1133, 1137, 1138, 1147, 1149, 1151, 1152, 1154, 1157, 1165. Sold for scrap in 1982: 1131, 1136, 1144, 1155, 1156, 1161, 1162, 1163, 1166, 1167.

Held for reserve outside Pier 72 area, (1990); 1101, 1110, 1124, 1125, 1127, 1141, 1143, 1169. Stored inside building: (1990) 1103, 1105, 1106, 1109, 1111, 1113, 1115, 1122, 1123, 1130, 1139, 1140, 1142, 1145, 1148, 1153, 1158, 1160, 1168, 1170.

1200-1299 Demonstrators #1220 and #1221 arrived in 1977 for test runs both with trolley poles. Returned to Boeing Vertol for refinements and sent back to Muni as #1212 and #1213 with pantographs. #1213 reverted to trolley poles in 1983 for Festival car backup operating on Market Street. In 1984, #1212 also to trolley poles for added backup. After 1984 summer season both back to pantographs and LRV subway service. In July 1989, #1212 (#1212A and 1255B) and #1294 (#1294B and 1297A) scrapped account accident damage. #1212B and #1225A became #1255. #1294A and #1297B became #1297. All others on active roster 1990.

The Billboard Cars

During World War II, and shortly thereafter, the Muni embarked on billboard ads on the sides of a number of their street cars, some of these colorful show pieces are shown on the next several pages.

MUNI #166, JUNE 19, 1945
Francis Stewart and Robert Skelton photo

MUNI #131, SEPTEMBER 15, 1947
Muni photo

MUNI #43
Black roof, silver sides,
first line in blue, second black.
Bert Ward photo

MUNI #188
Gray roof, blue lettering on yellow.
Bert Ward photo

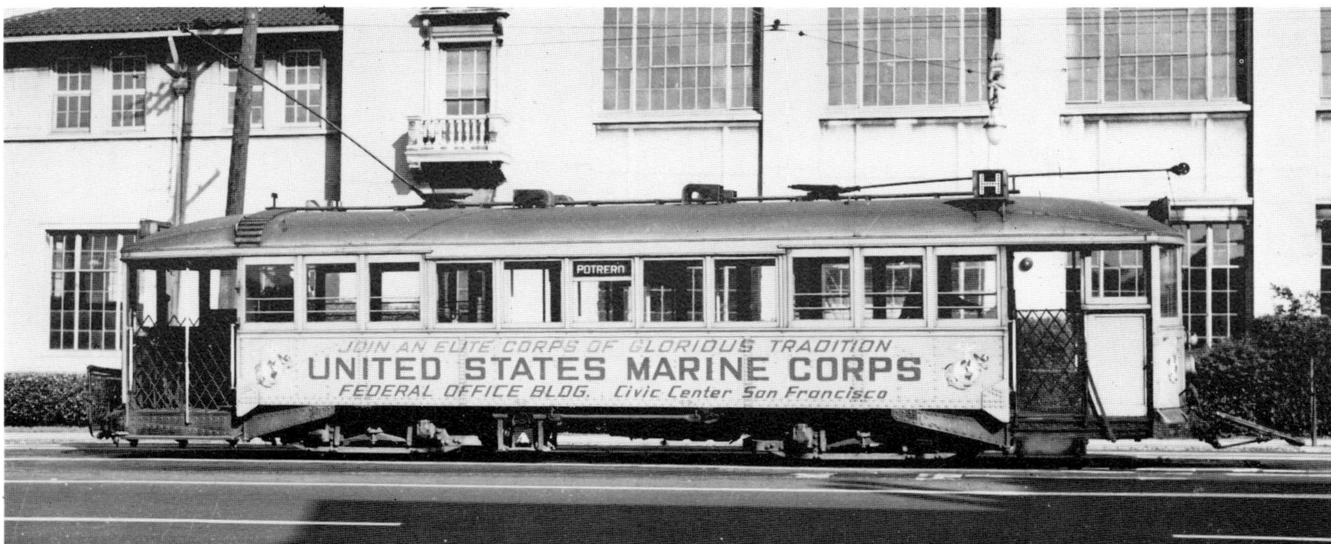

MUNI #141
Various blues on yellow.
Bert Ward photo

MUNI #86
Green and cream with blue lettering.
Art Lloyd photo

MUNI #148
Colors and date unknown.
Guido collection

MUNI #134
Blue and cream, ad colors unknown.
Tom Gray collection

MUNI #53
Red on white, gray roof.
Bert Ward photo

MUNI #118
Blue and cream.
Muni photo

MUNI #167, October 25, 1946
Cream, green and yellow.
Lettering in green and yellow.
Muni photo

EX MARKET #206, MAY 10, 1946
Black roof, silver side, blue letters.
Muni photo

EX MARKET #203
Blue and yellow
Muni photo

MUNI #148
Green roof with red stripe border below,
Green window posts.
Muni photo

Probably the World's best-dressed trolley trainees prepare to take nicely painted, blue and yellow, Muni #887 out for a lesson on December 1, 1945. It was one of the few ex Market Street Railway cars to receive the complete blue and yellow decor. Built at Elkton shops, it was ready for service, September 15, 1928. It lasted 20 years being retired on October 5, 1948. ***Muni photo.***

The "B" line was inaugurated to the Ocean Beach, June 25, 1913. Car #128 is shown on what was probably the "happiest" of Muni lines, with passengers headed for Playland and Chutes-At-The-Beach for some fun-filled hours. *Ted Wurm collection.*

CHAPTER 6

SAN FRANCISCO MUNICIPAL RAILWAY

ROUTES

Before the acquisition of the Market Street Railway in 1944 with its 25 street car lines, the city owned railway had a total of 15 lettered street car routes during its 32 years of existence. They were numbered in alphabetical sequence "A" through "O". An additional route, #32, was established in 1948 for a short duration.

This compilation gives the day the electric street car lines commenced operation and changes that took place. The final day of operation is also noted with the exception of lines J-K-L-M and N, which are in operation today (1990). The compilation for the Market Street Railway lines taken over by the Muni in 1944 are shown in the Market Street Railway Route Section.

Actually there were two "J" routes, the first along with the "G" and "I" lines were operated only during the Panama Pacific Exposition in the years 1915-1916. The second "J" route, known as the Church Street line, began operation in 1917 and is in operation today (1990). The letters "G" and "I" were never used again. The 32 line was placed in operation from the Ferry Loop, first during the peak hours and later during midday, to the turn in at Duboce, just below the San Francisco Mint, from March 14, 1948 to June 6, 1948. This route was necessary for patrons transferring from lines 5-6-7-21 and 31, which terminated at Market Street while the thoroughfare was being reconstructed from four tracks to two tracks.

You will note that all lines on Market Street ended at the Ferry Loop, until beginning of electric train service from the East Bay over the San Francisco-Oakland Bay Bridge in 1939. At that time certain lines were diverted or alternated to the new East Bay Terminal located at Mission Street between First and Fremont. On May 27, 1947, all cars were routed to the East Bay Terminal with the abandonment of tracks to the Ferry Loop below Fremont Street. The East Bay Terminal tracks were only used by Festival street cars after the PCC cars ended on September 19, 1982 with all service on the remaining five street cars shifting to LRV subway service on the same date.

GEARY-PARK
(Ferry Loop to 10th and Fulton)

From Ferry Loop on Market to Geary, 10th Ave, Fulton. (4.8 miles)

Start of street car operation (Inner terminal at Geary and Kearny .... December 28, 1912
(replaced old cable car line)
Inner terminal extended to Ferry Loop on Market. .... June 25, 1913
Last day of street car operation. .... December 5, 1932

Car #125 swings around the Ferry Loop, with the letter "A" in its route box, late 1910's. From the direction of the commuters it must be 5 pm as they head for the various ferry slips and their homes on the other side of the bay. ***Tom Gray collection.***

GEARY-OCEAN
(Ferry Loop to Ocean Beach)

From Ferry Loop on Market to Geary, 33rd Ave, Balboa, 45th Ave., Cabrillo to Great Highway (Ocean Beach) (7.06 miles).

Started as a shuttle on Geary between 10th and 33rd Ave.	*December 28, 1912*
Extended to Geary and Kearny.	*February 10, 1913*
Inner terminal extended to Ferry Loop on Market	*June 25, 1913*
Outer terminal extended from Geary on 33rd to Balboa, 45th, Cabrillo to Great Highway (Ocean Beach).	*June 25, 1913*
Loop installed at Ocean Beach.	*April 25, 1915*
Inner terminal alternate cars to East Bay Terminal.	*January 15, 1939*
Inner terminal all cars to East Bay Terminal	*June 1, 1941*
Inner terminal Geary and Kearny account Market Street track work	*April 9-June 2, 1949*
Last day of street car operation.	*December 29, 1956*

(Above) Car #208 at the outer terminal "Playland-at-the-Beach" in the year 1935. ***Stindt collection.*** **(Below) Car #147 swings into Geary from 33rd Avenue as it heads downtown.** ***Tom Gray collection.***

GEARY - CALIFORNIA
(Ferry Loop to 33rd and California)

From Ferry Loop to Geary, 2nd Ave., Cornwall, California to 33rd Ave. (5.91 miles).

Start of street car operation Ferry Loop to 13th & California	*February 19, 1915*
Outer terminal extended to 33rd and California	*March 28, 1915*
Inner terminal alternate cars to East Bay Terminal	*January 15, 1939*
Resume all cars to Ferry Loop	*January 1, 1941*
Inner terminal all cars to East Bay Terminal	*July 21, 1946*
Inner terminal Geary and Kearny account Market Str. track work	*April 9-June 2, 1949*
Outer terminal to 2nd and Cornwall	*September 26, 1949*
Last day of street car operation	*December 29, 1956*

(Above) Car #10 sports a brand new blue and yellow paint livery as it sits at the outer terminal at 33rd and California. ***Will Whittaker photo.*** **(Below) Ex Market car #644, renumbered from #244, in Muni green and cream colors with side wings, at the end of the "C" line at 33rd and California. Many Market cars were assigned to this route after the Muni take-over in 1944. Photo taken in 1950.** ***Bert Ward photo.***

GEARY - VAN NESS
(Ferry Loop to Presidio)

From Ferry Loop on Market to Geary, Van Ness, Union, Steiner, Greenwich, Private right-of-way to Presidio. (4.24 miles)

Start of street car operation from Ferry Loop on Market, to Geary, Van Ness, Chestnut, Scott (*), Greenwich, Steiner, Union, Franklin, Vallejo, Van Ness and return to Ferry Loop via Geary. (*) Known as Exposition Loop-cars would alternate in direction to Scott Street entrance during 1915 fair .... August 15, 1914
When Exposition ended outer terminal route changed to Van Ness, Vallejo, Franklin, Union, Steiner, Greenwich, Scott .... December 6, 1915
Outer terminal extended on Greenwich from Scott to Baker and joined "E" line to Presidio .... May 4, 1918
Track on Scott between Greenwich and Chestnut removed .... May 4, 1918
Track on Vallejo from Van Ness to Franklin to Union removed, cars then to Union at Van Ness ... July 22, 1919
Presidio loop installed .... December 8, 1919
Inner terminal alternate cars to East Bay Terminal .... January 15, 1939
Inner terminal for all cars East Bay Terminal .... June 1, 1941
Inner terminal for all cars to Ferry Loop .... July 21, 1946
Inner terminal for all cars East Bay Terminal-Ferry loop abandoned .... March 27, 1949
Inner terminal Geary and Kearny .... April 9-June 2, 1949
Last day of street car operation .... March 17, 1950

(Above) Car #52, coming off Presidio right-of-way, enters Greenwich Street at Lyon on its way downtown in the year 1947. ***Tom Gray photo.*** **(Below) Car #203 enters the Ferry Loop in 1948. Like the street car, the buildings in the background are gone, replaced with the Hyatt Regency and the Embarcadero Center buildings.** ***Tom Gray photo.***

UNION STREET
(Ferry to Presidio)

From Ferry, north terminal, Embarcadero, Washington (outbound), Jackson (inbound), Columbus, Union, Larkin, Vallejo, Franklin, Union, Baker, Greenwich, private right-of-way to Presidio. (3.77 miles).

Event	Date
Take over street car operation from Presidio & Ferries Railroad	*December 11, 1913*
Alternate operation from Ferry to Stockton and Market commenced	*January 24, 1916*
Alternate operation to Stockton and Market discontinued	*June 27, 1918*
Track on Vallejo and Van Ness to Franklin to Union removed, cars then into Union at Van Ness	*July 22, 1919*
Inner terminal changed to Market and Van Ness	*June 1, 1932*
Inner terminal to Ferry terminal resumed	*July 15, 1932*
Inner terminal cut back to Powell and Union	*March 10, 1947*
Last day of street car operation	*June 8, 1947*

(Above) Car #354 at Union and Mason, May 24, 1942 with Charlie's Grocery store to the left. ***Bert Ward photo.*** **(Below) Three "E" cars, 362-361-366, at Presidio terminal in the late 1930's.** ***Guido collection.***

STOCKTON STREET
(Stockton and Market to Scott and Chestnut)

On Stockton from Market to Columbus, North Point, Van Ness, Chestnut to Scott. (3.08 miles)

Start of street ca, operation to outer terminal Chestnut and Laguna .... December 29, 1914
Outer terminal extended to Scott on Chestnut .... September 11, 1916
Every 3rd car routed over "E" line to Ferry north terminal during Golden Gate International Exposition on Treasure Island 1939-1940
Inner terminal extended down Fourth to Townsend to Third (SP Depot) taking over in part old Market Street Ry #20 line. .... September 8, 1947
Inner terminal extended during peak hours to 2nd & Market via Third, Brannan, 2nd to Market replacing old Market Street Railway #41 line .... January 17, 1949
Inner terminal back to 3rd and Townsend .... December 10, 1949
Last day of street car operation .... January 19, 1951

(Above) Once in a while one of the center entrance "dinkies" would be assigned to the "F" line. Car #368 on Stockton having passed Sutter Street, year 1940. *Guido collection.* (Below) Car #36 swings from Stockton, to cross Market into Fourth on its way to the S.P. Depot in 1940. Notice stores that are no longer in existence. *Guido collection.*

EXPOSITION
(Stockton and Market to Presidio)

On Stockton from Market, Columbus, North Point, Van Ness, Chestnut, Scott, Union, Baker, Greenwich to Presidio.

Start of street car operation .... *February 20, 1915*
Last day of operation .... *September 1915*

Car #320 at Presidio ready for its trek to 4th and Market during the 1915 Exposition. ***Muni collection.***

POTRERO
(Fort Mason to Potrero and Army)

Fort Mason to Van Ness, 11th Street, Division, Potrero, to Army Street (4.66 miles)

Start of street car operation from Market on Van Ness to Bay	*August 15, 1914*
Extended across Market to 11th, Division, Potrero to 25th Street	*September 17, 1914*
(On Potrero from 18th to 25th joint use with Ocean Shore RR)	
Extended on private right-of-way into Fort Mason (U.S. Docks) from Bay St.	*December 5, 1914*
Extended from 25th to Army Street	*December 21, 1916*
Extended from Army Street 1/4 mile	*January 19, 1917*
Ocean Shore RR ends. Trackage to Muni on Potrero	*October 20, 1920*
Extended from Army via San Bruno Ave. to Arleta (former MSR #25 line)	*December 5, 1946*
Cut back from Arleta to Wilde Ave.	*June 30, 1947*
Fort Mason loop ends-Bay Street end of line	*January 15, 1948*
Army Street again established as end of line	*July 2, 1949*
Last day of street car operation	*March 17, 1950*

Car #53 on the Fort Mason loop in 1947. *Art Lloyd photo.*

(Above) Car #131 ambles along San Bruno Avenue, February 5, 1949. This section taken over from the old Market Street Railway route #25, December 5, 1946. ***Art Lloyd photo.*** **(Below) Hard to believe, but one of the old Market Street Jewetts on the "H" line! #404 (ex #104) at 11th and Market in 1947.** ***Tom Gray photo.***

EXPOSITION
(33rd and Geary to Chestnut and Scott)

On Geary from 33rd, to Van Ness, Chestnut, Scott, Greenwich, Steiner, Union, Franklin, Vallejo, to Van Ness and Return.

First day of street car operation . . . . *February 20, 1915*
Last day of operation (ran only three days) . . . . *February 22, 1915*

(first)

EXPOSITION
(Fort Mason to Ferry (north) via Columbus)

From Ferry North Terminal, Embarcadero, Washington (outbound), Jackson (inbound), Columbus, North Point, Van Ness to Fort Mason. (3.10 miles).

Start of street car operation . . . . *February 10, 1915*
Outer terminal extended to Scott and Chestnut . . . . *July 9, 1915*
Last day of street car operation . . . . *June 1, 1916*

(second)

CHURCH
(Ferry Loop to 30th & Church)

From Ferry Loop on Market to Church to 30th Street. (4.37 miles).

Start of street car operation from Van Ness on Market to Church and 30th (18th to 22nd private right-of-way) . . . . *August 11, 1917*
Inner terminal extended on Van Ness to Pine. . . . . *August 29, 1917*
Inner terminal on Van Ness to Pine discontinued . . . . *May 31, 1918*
Inner terminal on Market to Ferry Loop starts . . . . *June 1, 1918*
Inner terminal alternate cars to East Bay Terminal . . . . *January 15, 1939*
Inner terminal to Ferry Loop . . . . *January 1, 1941*
Account track reconstruction took over MSR #9 line from Market . . . . *March 27, 1946*
Return to regular route . . . . *November 11, 1946*
Inner terminal to East Bay Terminal. Ferry Loop abandoned. . . . . *March 27, 1949*
Trackage on Market between Duboce and Church discontinued with reroute on Duboce to Church account subway construction . . . . *December 3, 1972*
Light rail vehicles (subway) begin weekdays. PCC cars (surface) weekends . . . . *June 17, 1981*
Full LRV daily service and PCC cars end . . . . *September 19, 1982*

(''J'' line in service 1990)

Extension 30th and Church to San Jose and Ocean - 2 miles under construction (1990)

Car #101 climbs the grade in beautiful Dolores Park with San Francisco skyline in background. One of the picturesque settings along the Muni Railway. ***Tom Gray photo.***

(Above) Between 16th and Market on Church there was a four-track operation. Photo shows Market car #864 ready to swing into 16th from Church as Muni car #64 crosses the intersection heading downtown, March 17, 1946. ***Art Lloyd photo.*** **(Below) Muni PCC #1038 crosses 20th Street in the new Landor colorful paint livery, June 8, 1978.** ***Stindt photo.***

Parades on Market Street force rerouting of cars to Mission Street. Car #73 at Mission Ferry terminal during a summer day in 1949. (Below) LRV #1278 crosses 17th at Church heading outbound. ***Tom Gray photos.***

INGLESIDE
(Ferry Loop to Balboa Park BART Station)

From Ferry Loop on Market, Twin Peaks tunnel, West Portal, St. Francis Circle, Junipero Serra, Ocean, Balboa Park BART Station. (8.12 miles)

Start of street car operation from Pine on Van Ness to Market through Twin Peaks tunnel to St. Francis Circle. .... February 3, 1918
Inner Terminal on Van Ness to Pine discontinued .... May 31, 1918
Inner Terminal on Market to Ferry Loop begins .... June 1, 1918
Outer terminal extended from St. Francis Circle on Junipero Serra to Ocean, to Miramar (joint use MSR trackage). .... February 21, 1919
Sundays, holidays, alternate cars to 33rd and Taraval ("L" line) .... April 13, 1919
Outer terminal extended on Ocean to Brighton to Grafton .... May 18, 1919
Sundays, holidays, alternate cars extended to beach ("L" line) .... January 14, 1923
Sundays, holidays, alternate cars on "L" line discontinued .... October 21, 1923
Inner terminal alternate cars to East Bay Terminal .... January 15, 1939
Inner terminal to East Bay Terminal all cars .... January 1, 1941
Outer terminal alternate cars to Onondaga and Mission .... April 8, 1945
New outer terminal; Phelan Loop at Phelan and Ocean. Brighton from Ocean to Grafton discontinued .... May 18, 1952
Alternate cars to Onondaga and Mission ends .... October 10, 1952
Market between Duboce and 17th abandoned. New route off at Duboce to Church, 17th to Market and Twin Peaks tunnel begins .... December 3, 1972
Light Rail Vehicle (LRV) supplemental weekday service inaugurated from West Portal to Balboa Park BART station via Ocean Ave. .... April 23, 1979
LRV supplemental service ends. PCC cars new outer terminal, Balboa Park station (account track problems PCC cars shifted to Geneva car barn loop across the street) .... February 18, 1980
LRV service from Embarcadero subway station to St. Francis Circle starts weekdays with K and L crosstown route of PCC cars established between Geneva car barn and "L" end of line at Zoo. (No change in weekend PCC downtown service) .... June 11, 1980
PCC cars cut back to Phelan Loop on weekends .... October 3, 1980
K and L crosstown service ends .... December 16, 1980
Full LRV weekday service begins Embarcadero to Balboa Park .... December 17, 1980
Phelan Loop abandoned. Weekend PCC cars to Geneva Car Barn Loop .... March 17, 1981
Full LRV daily service begins. All PCC operation ends .... September 19, 1982

("K" line in service 1990)

When the old Market Street Railway #12 line was cut back to Geneva and Mission, April 4, 1945, alternate "K" line cars were extended to Onondaga and Mission Streets. Four days later, on old #12's tracks, car #148 is shown at the new terminus. *Art Lloyd photo.*

(Top) At St. Francis Circle car #209 on its outbound trek swings into Junipero Serra Blvd. from West Portal, 1949. *Tom Gray photo.* (Above) PCC car #1028 on the Phelan Loop shortly after this track was placed in service in 1951. *Will Whittaker photo.* (Below) To get two ex Toronto cars together in a photo was difficult, but to get them together on the same line was a rarity. #1187 and #1188 at Duboce and Market in 1978 on the "K" line *Stindt photo.*

(Above) "Magic Carpet" car #1002 at the outer terminal at Brighton and Grafton, June 7, 1942. Note 5c fare! *Art Lloyd photo.* (Below) On a summer day in 1979 LRV #1224 rolls along Ocean Avenue on outbound "K" run. *Tom Gray photo.*

TARAVAL
(Ferry Loop to Fleishhackers Zoo)

From Ferry Loop on Market through Twin Peaks tunnel, Ulloa, 15th Ave., Taraval, 46th Ave., Vicente, 47th Ave., Wawona (Zoo) and return on 46th to Taraval. (7.95 miles).

Start of street car operation from West Portal to Ulloa, 15th Ave., Taraval, to 33rd Ave. (20th-33rd United Railroad tracks) . . . . April 12, 1919
Outer terminal extended on Taraval from 33rd to 48th Ave. . . . . January 14, 1923
Inner terminal extended from West Portal through Twin Peaks tunnel, Market Street to Ferry Loop . . . . October 15, 1923
United Railroads discontinues 20th-33rd section - to Muni Ownership . . . . Late 1927
Outer terminal extended on 46th from Taraval to Vicente, 47th Ave., Wawona (Zoo) return to 46th to Taraval . . . . September 15, 1937
Inner terminal alternate cars to East Bay Terminal . . . . January 15, 1939
Inner terminal all cars to Ferry Loop . . . . January 1, 1941
Inner terminal all cars to East Bay Terminal . . . . June 6, 1948
Market between Duboce and 17th abandoned. New route off at Duboce to Church, 17th to Market and Twin Peaks tunnel . . . . December 3, 1972
PCC cars K-L line shuttle starts to connect with LRV cars at West Portal . . . . June 11, 1980
PCC K-L line shuttle ends . . . . December 16, 1980
Full weekday LRV subway service starts. PCC weekends (surface) . . . . December 17, 1980
All operation of PCC cars ends. Full LRV service . . . . September 19, 1982
("L" line in service 1990)

Car #77 in brand new blue and yellow decor travels along Taraval near 43rd Avenue, March March 7, 1942. Today (1990) this area is completely built over with homes and apartments. ***Will Whittaker photo.***

(Above) ''L'' car #109 outbound at First and Market with ''J'' car #96 inbound and ex Market car #228 on the ''3'' line in the background, 1949. *Tom Gray photo.* (Below) ''Magic Carpet'' car #1001 at Taraval and 35th Avenue, May 1952 *Will Whittaker photo.*

(Above) Car #1181 is packed with homebound commuters on a summer day in 1976 on outer Market Street near Duboce. (Below) LRV #1250 and #1310 swing from Taraval into 46th Avenue heading for the terminus at 47th and Wawona, June 27, 1989. ***Both Stindt photos.***

OCEAN VIEW
(Ferry Loop to Geneva and San Jose Avenue)

From Ferry Loop on Market through Twin Peaks tunnel, West Portal, St. Francis Circle, private right-of-way, 19th Ave., Randolph, Orizaba, Broad, San Jose Ave., to Geneva (car barn turn around). (9.25 miles).

Start of street car service Plymouth and Broad to St. Francis Circle	*October 6, 1925*
Extended St. Francis Circle to Ferry Loop	*October 31, 1927*
Re-established as a shuttle St. Francis Circle to Broad and Plymouth	*February 27, 1928*
Entire line discontinued	*August 6, 1939*
Resumed full length	*December 17, 1944*
Inner terminal to East Bay Terminal	*June 6, 1948*
Market between Duboce and 17th abandoned. New route off at Duboce to Church, 17th, to Market and Twin Peaks tunnel	*December 3, 1972*
Entire line discontinued a/c rerailing Twin Peaks tunnel and the line itself	*January 13, 1974*
Resumed full length	*December 20, 1978*
Outer terminal extended via San Jose Ave. to Balboa Park BART station connecting with K line tracks	*August 30, 1980*
Outer terminal cut back to Plymouth and Broad account PCC cars track problems at Balboa Park	*October 3, 1980*
Full length subway LRV service weekdays to Balboa BART station with PCC cars to Plymouth and Broad weekends	*December 17, 1980*
All operation of PCC cars end. Full LRV service (outer terminal later changed to looping Geneva Car Barn)	*September 19, 1982*

("M" line in service 1990)

Car #42 has just crossed Eucalyptus Drive and is about to enter 19th Avenue right-of-way, 1939. ***Stindt collection.***

(Above) When operated as a shuttle between St. Francis Circle and Plymouth and Broad, the "Arnold" cars were assigned during the years 1928-1939. Car #43 ambles along 19th Avenue in May 1939, Today (1990) this area is filled with homes and San Francisco State College on the left. *Will Whittaker photo.* (Below) PCC car #1102 emerges from Twin Peaks tunnel. The car was totaled in a mishap with a truck in 1972. *Stindt collection.*

(Above) PCC car #1145 in Landor livery curves into Broad from Orizaba and soon will be at its outer terminal at Plymouth. (Below) LRV #1271 and #1241 have gone through the loop in Geneva barn and pause for passengers in front of the old Geneva office building, October 1988. ***Both Stindt photos.***

JUDAH

From Ferry Loop on Market to Duboce, Sunset tunnel, Carl, Arguello, Irving, 9th Ave., Judah to La Playa (Ocean Beach.) (7.06 miles)

Start of street car operation	*October 21, 1928*
Inner terminal alternate cars to East Bay Terminal	*January 15, 1939*
Inner terminal all cars to East Bay Terminal	*January 1, 1941*
Temporary trackage Duboce off Market to Church for subway construction.	*December 3, 1972*
(Temporary tracks remain for Festival car storage)	
LRV subway service weekdays full time. PCC cars weekends	*February 19, 1980*
PCC street cars end. Full LRV subway service daily	*September 19, 1982*

("N" line in service 1990)

Car #67 at outer terminal at Judah and La Playa, (Below) PCC car #1016 in front of Southern Pacific Building, 65 Market Street, shortly after its arrival in 1951. ***Both Guido collection.***

(Above) PCC car #1107 swings around the loop at outer "N" terminal, October 2, 1978. (Below) Two LRV's with #1221 in the lead near end of "N" line on Judah not far from La Playa, June 27, 1989. ***Both Stindt photos.***

VAN NESS

From Ferries, North Terminal, Embarcadero, Washington (Outbound), Jackson (inbound), Columbus, Union, Larkin, Vallejo to Van Ness.

Start of street car operation .... *June 1, 1932*
Last day of operation .... *July 15, 1932*

Car #371, July 4, 1932, on the short-lived "O" line. ***Smallwood collection.***

MARKET-DUBOCE
(Ferry Loop to Duboce and Market)

From Ferry Loop on Market to Duboce (below San Francisco Mint) (2.53 miles).

Start of street car operation .... *March 14, 1948*
Last day of street car operation .... *June 6, 1948*

Ex Market car #698 (ex #298) at Duboce turn-back off Market Street, May 1948. ***Bert Ward photo.***

CHAPTER 7

MISCELLANEOUS

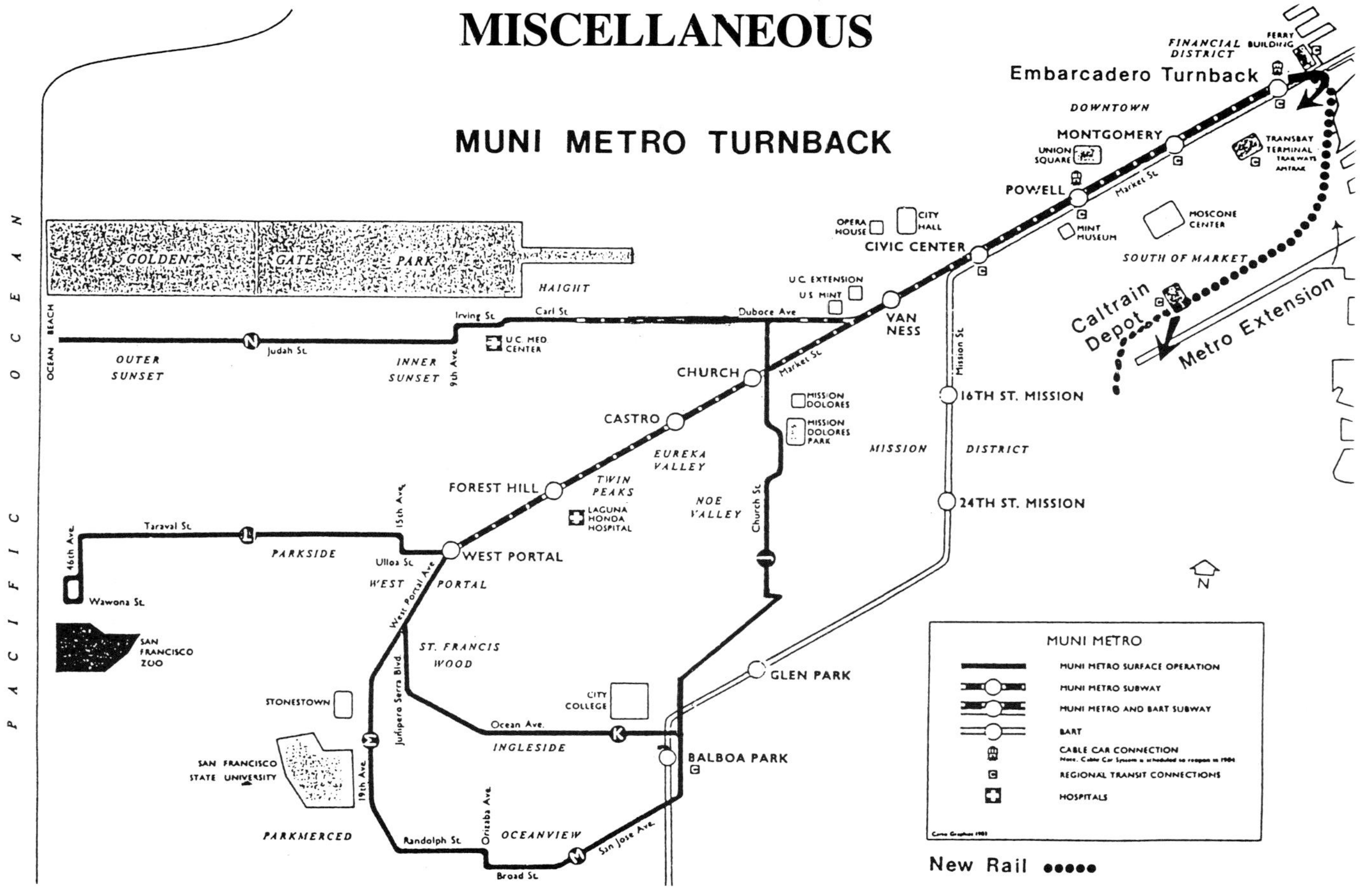

MUNI METRO TURNBACK

Embarcadero Turnback
FINANCIAL DISTRICT
FERRY BUILDING
DOWNTOWN
MONTGOMERY
UNION SQUARE
TRANSBAY TERMINAL
POWELL
MINT MUSEUM
MOSCONE CENTER
OPERA HOUSE
CITY HALL
CIVIC CENTER
SOUTH OF MARKET
Caltrain Depot
Metro Extension
U.C. EXTENSION
US MINT
VAN NESS
GOLDEN GATE PARK
HAIGHT
Irving St.
Carl St.
Duboce Ave.
U.C. MED CENTER
Judah St.
OUTER SUNSET
INNER SUNSET
9th Ave.
OCEAN BEACH
CHURCH
Market St.
Mission St.
16TH ST. MISSION
MISSION DOLORES
MISSION DOLORES PARK
CASTRO
EUREKA VALLEY
MISSION
DISTRICT
FOREST HILL
TWIN PEAKS
LAGUNA HONDA HOSPITAL
NOE VALLEY
Church St.
24TH ST. MISSION
15th Ave.
Taraval St.
46th Ave.
PARKSIDE
Ulloa St.
WEST PORTAL
Wawona St.
SAN FRANCISCO ZOO
West Portal Ave.
ST. FRANCIS WOOD
GLEN PARK
STONESTOWN
Junipero Serra Blvd.
CITY COLLEGE
Ocean Ave.
INGLESIDE
BALBOA PARK
SAN FRANCISCO STATE UNIVERSITY
19th Ave.
PARKMERCED
Orizaba Ave.
Randolph St.
OCEANVIEW
San Jose Ave.
Broad St.
PACIFIC OCEAN

MUNI METRO
MUNI METRO SURFACE OPERATION
MUNI METRO SUBWAY
MUNI METRO AND BART SUBWAY
BART
CABLE CAR CONNECTION
REGIONAL TRANSIT CONNECTIONS
HOSPITALS

New Rail ●●●●●

(Above) Map shows present Muni lines in San Francisco. Dotted line from Ferry Building area to Mission Bay is planned for mid 1990's. The Market Street subway will surface along the Embarcadero between Mission and Folsom, thence on private right-of-way to King Street and to 7th Street in the Mission Bay development project.

(Right) The Market Street "F" line is planned to commence in 1993. Broken line shows future expansion planned to Fishermen's Wharf area, Embarcadero, Jefferson, loop into Jones and back on Beach and return on the Embarcadero to Market.

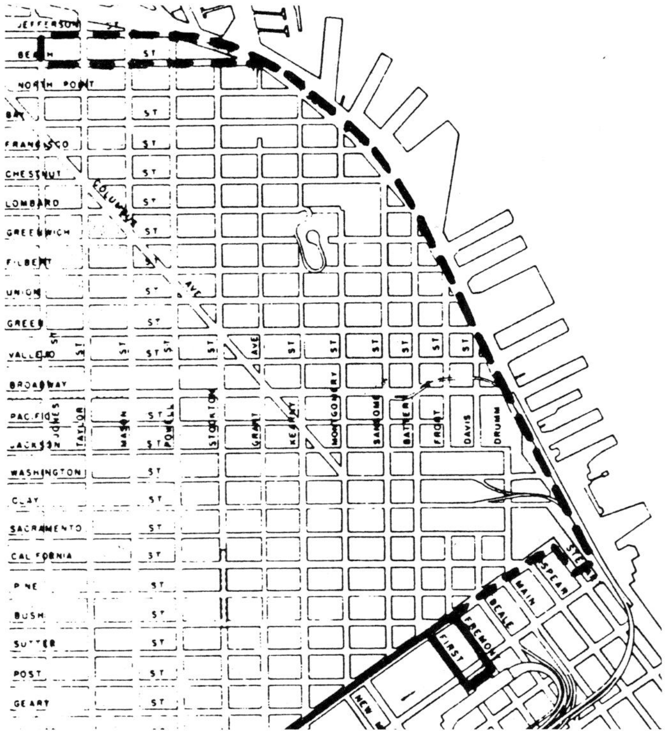

SPECIAL
TAKE NEXT CAR
ENTER AT REAR

Festival Street Cars

When the famed cable system was shut down over a two-year period, 1982-1984, for complete rebuilding of all cable car lines including the historic cable car powerhouse, the city fathers headed by Mayor Dianne Feinstein came up with the idea of a trolley festival of old street cars operating on Market Street during the summer months. The inauguration took place with much fanfare, June 21, 1983. Leading the festive parade of old cars was Muni #1, built in 1912, which had been saved and restored to its former elegance in 1962, followed by a parade of cars from various cities and several countries. Included were #122 and #189 from Portugal (owned by Portland, Oregon), #503 from Portland (owned by Oregon Electric Society), #648, Melbourne, Australia, #226, Blackpool, England and Muni #178 (all three owned by the Western Railway Museum, Rio Vista, California), Muni "iron monster" #130, Muni PCC #1128 as St. Louis Public Service car #1704, Muni PCC #1040 and Muni LRV #1213 with trolley poles. Milwaukee #978 arrived in such poor condition that it never operated and was returned. Total cars in operation - eleven. The trolley festival was an outstanding success and would be scheduled each summer in the foreseeable future. Former Market Street Railway single truck car #578 was restored to its original appearance by Muni in 1956, but retained only for historical observances account it is equipped only with hand braking.

In 1984, Muni PCC #1006 and LRV #1212 with trolley poles were added along with the following new additions: Milan, Italy car #1834; Vera Cruz, Mexico #001 and Hamburg, Germany car #3557. At the end of the summer season Portugal Car #122 was returned to Portland and the two LRV's #1212 and #1213 were returned to subway service with their pantographs reinstalled. Total operating in 1984 -sixteen.

In 1985, same as end of 1984 excluding returned cars. When season concluded, #178 and Blackpool #226 were returned to Western Railway Museum, Portland car #503 back to Portland and Mexico car #001 back to Mexico. Total operating in summer of 1985 - thirteen.

In 1986, Hiroshima, Japan, car #578 and Blackpool, England, car #228 were added and Melbourne car #648 returned to Western Railway Museum. Total operating during summer months - eleven. Old Market Street Railway body #798 arrived as did Milan, Italy, suburban car #96. #798 would have to be completely rebuilt and Milan car needed extensive repairs. A wye was installed at Noe and 17th Streets to turn one-man festival cars. Henceforth, one-man cars will no longer have to go out the "N" line to 30th Avenue for turning purposes.

In 1987, Melbourne, Australia, cars #496 and #586 joined the fleet, but car #586 did not operate account repairs needed. Also added was Russian car #106. Total operating during 1987 summer - twelve. Osaka, Japan, car #151 also arrived and was stored at Metro car barn. Muni did not take ownership until February 28, 1989, from the Railway Corporate Assembly group. Also, in 1987, on a test basis with funds provided by the Fisherman's Wharf merchants, the Muni, on Fridays and Saturdays, September 11th to October 17th, operated two vintage cars, San Francisco car #578 and Portugal car #189 from the Ferry Building on old Belt Line tracks to Pier 39. Power was from a small 4-wheel electric generator unit attached to the rear of the cars. The test was successful with good patronage. However, financial support was not forthcoming for its continuance in following years. Seven of the festival cars had one final operation in 1987 during the celebration of Muni's 75 anniversary on December 28th. The following cars took part: #1, #130, #1006, #1040, Milan #1834, Hamburg #3557 and Russian #106.

During the summer months of 1988 and 1989 there was no city festival car operation due to construction work on Market Street. However, during the winter months with tracks in place, local transit historical groups on several occasions operated one day trips with one or several of the historical car fleet.

On June 27, 1989 car body #798 was trucked to the Deul Correctional Facility at Tracy, California, where inmates will restore the car to its former elegance. No time has been set for completion.

During July, 1989, Johnstown Traction street car #351 arrived at Muni Metro, Geneva yard and Los Angeles Railway car #1435 at Pier 72. #351 will probably see Festival car service after some extensive overhaul, but #1435 being of different gauge may become a parts car. The two units were for many years at Freestone, California, where a museum was planned, but did not materialize. The cars were obtained by the Market Street Railway club.

As this book goes to press the first part of June, 1990, the mayor has not authorized funding for Festival car operation in the summer of 1990, so none is planned at this writing. However, the Festival cars are available for charter hire.

The following are Festival cars owned by the San Francisco Municipal Railway, June 1, 1990:

Muni #1
Muni #130
Muni #1006
Muni #1040
Muni #578 ex Market St. Ry.
St. Louis #1704, ex Muni #1128
Blackpool, England #228
Melbourne, Australia #496
Melbourne, Australia #586
Milan, Italy #96
Milan, Italy #1834
Osaka, Japan #151
Hiroshima, Japan #578
Portugal #189
Orel, Russia #106
Market St. Ry #798
Johnstown, Penna. #351
(still owned by Market St. Ry. Club)
Toronto, Canada PCC #4472
(Arrived April 3, 1990, still owned by Toronto Transit Co.)

(Left) Mayor Dianne Feinstein, who gave her blessing to the Festival car service on Market Street a year earlier, inaugurates with much enthusiasm the second year of the historic cars, June 7, 1984. With the Mayor sharing the colorful occasion is Muni conductor Reno Bini. There were eleven cars in the festive parade. *Carmen Magana, (SFPUC) Muni collection.*

Decorated with balloons and flags, Muni #1, the leader of the Festival car fleet, rolls outbound on Market Street just having passed Third Street, May 14, 1987. The car was built by W. L. Holman Company in 1912. It was saved as a historical car in 1956. *Bill Owyang (SFPUC) Muni collection.*

During the summer months of 1983-1984 LRV #1213 with trolley poles was pressed into Festival car service. Sister car #1212 joined the operation in 1984 for one year. They were returned to subway service. Considered a rare photo, as LRV's on the surface of Market Street may never occur again. Outbound at 8th and Market. *Will Whittaker photo.*

Another popular car is the Hamburg, Germany car #3557, which came into the Festival car fleet in 1984. Muni owned. Outbound ready to turn into Duboce. San Francisco Mint in the background. In the year 1987, *Stindt photo.*

Melbourne, Australia #496 about to enter Market Street at Buchanan and Duboce in the summer of 1987. *Stindt photo.*

Milan, Italy car #1834 joined the Festival service in 1984 and is owned by the Muni. Another popular car, it has seen service each year of operation and on many charter movements. Photo near the intersection of Church and Duboce. *Stindt photo.*

Open car #228 from Blackpool, England is the most popular. Excellent to see the skyscrapers along Market Street. Came into Muni ownership in 1986. A like car, #226, owned by Bay Area Electric Railroad Association loaned their open car to the City in 1983, but was returned to them at the conclusion of the 1985 season. *Stindt photo.*

In 1987 this single truck car, #106 from Orel, Russia, joined the Festival car fleet. With balloons to give it a festive look the outbound car passes Powell Street, the terminus of the Powell cable lines, November 21, 1989. *Carmen Magana (SFPUC). Muni collection.*

On Fridays and Saturdays, September 11 to October 17, 1987, Pier 39 sponsored Festival car service between the Ferry Building and Pier 39 on abandoned Belt Line tracks. The two historical street cars, Portugal #189 and Muni single trucker #578 (historical car shown), obtained their power from a trailing motor-generator. September 26, 1987. *Stindt photo.*

Oddities

(Top) Muni car #76 on "N" line, in front of Pier 1, during an Admission Day (California to the Union, 1850) parade. Car was shunted over to the "E" line in a rare occurrence, September 9, 1939. ***Will Whittaker photo.*** (Center) On a farewell excursion of Market Street Railway cars, the Bay Area Electric Railroad Association, which owned car #974 donated to the group by the railway, makes a final tour of lines, March 19, 1950. A track was maintained to the cable car barn at Washington – Mason to haul cable cars on flat cars to Elkton shops for heavy repairs. On the return from the cable car barn this photo showns car #974 swinging from Mason into Broadway. Note #60, a cable car route, in the indicator box along with a dash sign prepared for the occasion by Richard Schlaich, prominent transist historian. Sadly #974 never made it to the Bay Area Electric Trolley farm at Rio Vista. Destroyed by fire upon restoration. ***Stindt photo.*** (Below) Sacramento Northern Birney car #62 in front of the Matson Building at 215 Market Street. All buildings in center background are gone and in their place is the Federal Reserve Bank Building. The Birney car was brought to San Francisco for this one-day excursion, January 21, 1951 by the Bay Area Electric Railroad Association who sponsored the trip. The car traversed several of the Muni lines. Other than today's Festival cars one of the few times an outside car has operated on Municipal Railway tracks. ***Stindt photo.***

INDEX

San Francisco's Other Municipal Railway

Hetch Hetchy Railroad railcars #20 and #19 await passengers at the Mather station. 59 miles to the west and 3,585 feet lower in elevation, passengers could transfer to the Sierra Railway, to continue their journey. *Hubbard collection.*

Far from the crowded city, San Francisco's other municipal railway ran in the mountains of Tuolumne County, with steam powered trains, and small railcars for most of the passenger service. The railcars had the same gray paint scheme as their city cousins, the electric trolley cars, even the heralds were similar with a large "SF" predominating. The Hetch Hetchy Railroad was constructed to allow the building of O'Shaughnessy Dam, a part of the City of San Francisco's vast water and power project, which provided lower-cost electricity, and probably was instrumental in the preservation of electric-powered transit in the city.

PRODUCTION NOTES
This book produced by
Al Rose—Publications
Modesto, California 95353-3033
Text type: English Times
Typesetting: Kelly Sears and Ernie Hahn, Jr.
Display face: Destination Box Gothic
Presswork; Tom Hoefer
Printing: Modesto Printing Co.
Binding: Cardoza-James Binding Co., San Francisco
Text paper: Productolith, Sirroco Finish, Basis 80

M
OCEANVIEW
San Francisco Examiner
EXIT